THEORIES

OF

PARALLELISM

THEORIES

OF

PARALLELISM

AN HISTORICAL CRITIQUE

BY

WILLIAM BARRETT FRANKLAND

BOOKS FOR LIBRARIES PRESS
FREEPORT, NEW YORK

First Published 1910
Reprinted 1972

Library of Congress Cataloging in Publication Data

Frankland, Francis William Barrett, 1875-
   Theories of parallelism.

   Reprint of the 1910 ed.
   1. Parallels (Geometry). I. Title.
QA681.F8 1972   516'.15   72-7224
ISBN 0-8369-6931-6

PRINTED IN THE UNITED STATES OF AMERICA

IN PIAM MEMORIAM

ELIZABETHAE DE BURGH

APOLOGY

HAEC hactenus... Some years ago I made use of this expression incidentally in the course of my annotated edition of the *First Book of Euclid's Elements,* with reference to an historical sketch of the *Theory of Parallelism.* After much hesitation and with much diffidence, somewhat augmented by the appearance (after the first draft of this little volume had been prepared) of Dr Heath's most learned and elaborate *Thirteen Books of Euclid's Elements,* I have here tried to disburden conscience and memory by drawing up in chronological order my notes on the treatment of parallelism by about 40 Geometers of rank. Except for the last generation, I believe that these 40 names are the most noteworthy throughout twenty-two centuries in this connexion. As is well known, any theory of parallelism is not an isolated fragment of geometrical research, but must be capable of supporting the whole superstructure of the Science of Space. And the historical study of this matter is interesting, not least because it displays, in a manner partly amusing and partly pathetic, the dulnesses, limitations, prejudices and aberrations of professedly logical minds. Frail and imperfect demonstrations were once viewed with considerable complacency. Up to the middle of last century the treatment of parallelism was a favourite lurking-place for paralogisms. Wonderful indeed is the serene illumination of Truth by which the student works in this twentieth century. Compared with it, the Renascence was only a stirring and awakening out of sleep in the dim twilight of the early dawn. If it is not impertinent in me to suggest it, we seem to be finding the Balance of Truth.

W. B. F.

WRAWBY VICARAGE, LINCOLNSHIRE.
Septuagesima, 1909.

CONTENTS

INTRODUCTION

A BRIEF preliminary investigation of the bases of Geometry is necessary in order to furnish the means of testing the various Theories of Parallelism with which we shall deal. Knowing, for instance, whether the enunciation of a proposition is correct or incorrect, we know where most especially to search for mistakes of reasoning; and a careful study of the following Introduction should therefore make it a pleasurable task to criticise the work of the earlier Geometers. It will be observed that this short Introduction is not Euclidean in style nor elementary in method; nor again is it in itself thoroughly complete and satisfactory. On the one hand, the student interested in the future rather than the past of Geometry will turn to the masterly summaries in Dr Whitehead's two tracts (*The Axioms of Projective Geometry,* 1906; *The Axioms of Descriptive Geometry,* 1907; Cambridge). On the other hand, a strictly Euclidean exposition of the Fundamental Theorem of Geometry has been given in the Appendix to *Euclid Book I with a Commentary* (Cambridge, 1902); and the line of thought projected by Meikle, Kelland and Chrystal has been successfully followed out by Dr Manning (*Non-Euclidean Geometry,* Boston, 1901). However, the ensuing discussion will supply what is indispensable for critical purposes in this book. Some things in it, and in the Additional Notes at the end, may perhaps be called original work. Biographical information will be found in the pages of Mr Rouse Ball's *History of Mathematics* or Dr Cantor's *Geschichte der Mathematik.*

Without further preface let us assume that *straight lines* are freely applicable to themselves and to one another; and that there is a *plane* in which they are freely moveable; and let us investigate the *parallelism* of such straight lines in such an even plane. The principal theorem thus obtained may be allowed to accredit itself after the fashion in which the diamond approves itself the hardest stone. Whatever defects our proof of it may possess, its credentials have been shown by Beltrami to be irreproachable (below, page 48).

This Principal Theorem of Plane Geometry is as follows:

If two polygons are called equal in *area* when one can be dissected into triangles which can be pieced together to cover the other exactly; and if, in the uncertainty (apart from prejudice) about the angle-sum of any triangle being precisely π, we define the *divergence* of a polygon having n sides to be the difference between its angle-sum and $(n-2)\pi$; then *the area of any polygon is proportional to its divergence* (Hilbert).

For a proof of this, consider first this Lemma:

In any compact agglomeration of rectilinear cells in the plane, if ν is the number of the cells, σ the number of vertices, and ϖ the number of walls, then $\sigma + \nu = \varpi + 1$.

For if a broken line of ζ rectilinear pieces be introduced to connect two vertices of any cell, σ is increased by $\zeta - 1$, ν by 1, and ϖ by ζ. This being always true, and the equation $\sigma + \nu = \varpi + 1$ holding good for the external boundary, this same equation is always true.

Hence it follows that the divergence of the boundary of the agglomeration is equal to the sum of the divergences of the individual cells composing it. For if S be the angle-sum of the external boundary, supposed a polygon of n sides; and if $s_1, s_2 \ldots s_\nu$ are the angle-sums of the ν cells, of which the sides number $p_1, p_2 \ldots p_\nu$ respectively, then

sum of divergences of cells
$$= \Sigma \left\{ s_\nu - (p_\nu - 2)\pi \right\}$$
$$= S + (\sigma - n)2\pi - \pi\Sigma p_\nu + 2\nu\pi$$
$$= S + (\sigma - n + \nu)2\pi - \pi(2\varpi - n)$$
$$= S - (n-2)\pi$$
$$= \text{divergence of external boundary of agglomeration.}$$

Thus polygons of equal area have equal divergence. Hence with any area is associated a divergence. Let Δ be the area associated with the divergence δ. We may then write $\Delta = f(\delta)$; and as there is no reason to doubt the applicability of Euclidean Geometry to infinitesimal areas, Δ is a continuous function of δ. But, considering an agglomeration of two cells only, with divergences δ and ϵ,

$$f(\delta + \epsilon) = f(\delta) + f(\epsilon).$$

Differentiating for δ,

$$f'(\delta + \epsilon) = f'(\delta).$$

Hence $f'(\delta)$ is a constant, the same for every polygon, say A. Therefore, by integration for δ,

$$f(\delta) = A\delta + B,$$

where A and B are constant over the whole plane.

I.e. $\quad \Delta = A\delta + B.$

But when $\Delta \to 0$, $\delta \to 0$ also; for the geometry of an infinitesimal area can be accepted as Euclidean.

Thus $\qquad\qquad \Delta = A\delta,$

i.e. Area is proportional to Divergence.

According to the value of A for the plane, there are thus suggested three *Hypotheses* of equal rank, for A may be positive, or negative, or even (in the extreme case) infinite. In these cases $\delta > 0$, $\delta < 0$, or $\delta = 0$, throughout the plane. Accordingly the Geometry of the Plane may be either *Elliptic*, or *Hyperbolic*, or *Parabolic*; and for these three mutually exclusive Hypotheses, the angle-sum of a triangle is greater than, or is less than, or is equal to π, respectively. It may be said that the irrefragable demonstration of this Theorem is the greatest triumph ever won by Geometrical Science.

We can now prove that *for the elliptic, parabolic, and hyperbolic hypotheses, there are no, one and two parallels,* respectively, to any given straight line through any given point. For let M be the given point, and BB' the given straight line.

Draw MN perpendicular to BB', and AMA' perpendicular to MN. Within the angle AMN let a straight line through M, meeting NB in P, begin to rotate from MN towards MA. Then,

(i) *for the elliptic hypothesis, there are no parallels.*

For the area of the triangle MPN is proportional to the divergence of that triangle; say,

$$\triangle MPN = k^2 (\angle MNP + \angle MPN + \angle NMP - \pi)$$
$$= k^2 (\angle MPN - \angle AMP);$$

so that $\angle MPN > \angle AMP$; and as MP rotates further, and $\triangle MPN$ increases in area, the difference $\angle MPN - \angle AMP$ increases. Hence when $\angle AMP$ reaches zero, $\angle MPN$ is finite still; and therefore MP continues to intersect NB, even in the position MA. Thus for the elliptic hypothesis there are no parallels.

Next,

(ii) *for the parabolic hypothesis, there is one duplex parallel.*

For in this special case the divergence of the triangle MPN is zero. Thus $\angle MPN = \angle AMP$; and as MP rotates into the position MA, and $\angle AMP$ decreases to zero, so also does $\angle MPN$ *pari passu* decrease to zero. Therefore MA is parallel to NB (see Corollary below). And likewise MA' is parallel to NB'. But AMA' is one straight line; and so there is one duplex parallel for the parabolic hypothesis.

Lastly,

(iii) *for the hyperbolic hypothesis, there are two parallels.*

For the area of the triangle MPN is proportional to the divergence of that triangle; say,

$$\triangle MPN = K^2 (\pi - \angle MNP - \angle MPN - \angle NMP)$$
$$= K^2 (\angle AMP - \angle MPN);$$

so that $\angle MPN < \angle AMP$; and as MP rotates, and $\triangle MPN$ increases in area, the difference $\angle AMP - \angle MPN$ increases. Hence before $\angle AMP$ reaches zero, $\angle MPN$ has vanished; and therefore (see Corollary below) MP is parallel to NB in some position MH within the angle NMA. Similarly there is another distinct parallel MH' within the angle NMA'. Thus for the hyperbolic hypothesis there are two parallels.

To strengthen this argument, we choose a suitable definition of *parallelism,* and deduce a Corollary in the manner of Lobachewski.

DEFINITION. A *parallel* to a given straight line through a given point is that straight line which never intersects the given straight line, however far both are produced in the direction of parallelism, *whereas* any other straight line drawn through the given point, and inside the parallel, does intersect the given straight line.

COROLLARY. The angle MPN decreases to zero as MP becomes parallel to NB.

We will show that if ϵ be any assigned angle, however small, then $\angle MPN < \epsilon$, before MP reaches the position of parallelism. Let MN be perpendicular to BNB', as usual, and let MH be as before the parallel to NB through M; and let MP make with MH on the inside an angle ϵ. Then, by the definition of parallelism, MP meets NB, say at P. Along NB measure off $PQ = PM$. Then MQ is a straight line meeting NB, and lying within the angle PMH. But by an indubitable proposition, $\angle MQP = \angle QMP < \epsilon$. Thus a straight line MQ has been found such that $\angle MQN < \epsilon$, however small ϵ may be.

This Corollary is of course intended for the parabolic and hyperbolic hypotheses only.

With whatever defects, this discussion of Parallelism is sufficient in this place. It is necessary also to observe carefully the nature of *equidistants* to a given straight line. So far from equidistants being identical with parallels, *equidistants are not rectilinear,* save in the infinitely special case of the parabolic hypothesis.

Consider two straight lines MA, NB which possess a common perpendicular MN. Let a perpendicular to NB at any point Q meet MA in P. Then the angle MPQ is not

right, except for the parabolic hypothesis; for the elliptic
or hyperbolic hypotheses, it is obtuse or acute respectively.
Furthermore, as Q moves along NB, and area $PQNM$ increases,
the angle MPQ continually increases, decreases, or remains the
same, according as the elliptic, hyperbolic, or parabolic hypothesis holds good, respectively. It will also be useful to prove
(as in the Appendix to *Euclid Book I with a Commentary*) that
the length of the perpendicular PQ decreases, increases, or
remains the same, respectively.

PROPOSITION. If AM, BN are straight lines, to which MN is
a common perpendicular; and as Q moves in NB from N to B,
PQ is always drawn perpendicular to NB to meet MA in P;
then according as the elliptic, parabolic, or hyperbolic hypothesis is maintained, the length of PQ continually decreases,
remains the same, or increases, respectively.

For suppose P_1Q_1, P_2Q_2, P_3Q_3 to be three positions of PQ
as Q moves from N towards B. If P_2Q_2 is greater than P_1Q_1
and P_3Q_3, or again if P_2Q_2 is less than both the others, contrary
to the enunciation, then it will be possible to find two positions
of PQ, namely, pq between P_1Q_1 and P_2Q_2, and $p'q'$ between
P_2Q_2 and P_3Q_3, such that pq and $p'q'$ are of equal length
(Principle of Continuity).

Consider now nothing else but the quadrilateral $pqq'p'$ in
which angles q, q' are right, and the sides pq, $p'q'$ equal. Bisect
qq' in k, and draw kh perpendicular to qq' to meet pp' in h.
Fold the quadrilateral $pqq'p'$ about hk, so that kq covers kq'.
Then qp covers $q'p'$. And since h and p have now the positions
h and p', hp covers hp'. Hence the angles khp and khp' are
equal; and therefore the angle khp is right.

Hence the divergence of the quadrilateral $MhkN$ is zero;
and therefore the area/divergence constant is infinite; and so
the geometry of the plane is parabolic, and all the perpendiculars PQ equal, contrary to supposition. Thus in the
elliptic and hyperbolic hypotheses the length of PQ continually
decreases and increases, respectively.

It is in fact evident that PQ decreases for the elliptic
hypothesis, for at finite distance along NB it vanishes. And

it should be noted, that for the hyperbolic hypothesis PQ becomes infinite at finite distance from MN; indeed, considerations of area and divergence suggest that $\angle MPQ$ must presently vanish. If b, x, y are the lengths of MN, NQ, QP, then for the elliptic hypothesis,

$$\tan \frac{y}{k} = \cos \frac{x}{k} \tan \frac{b}{k};$$

and for the hyperbolic hypothesis,

$$\tanh \frac{y}{K} = \cosh \frac{x}{K} \tanh \frac{b}{K},$$

so that y is infinite for

$$\cosh \frac{x}{K} = \coth \frac{b}{K}.$$

To these results may be added the following, of which satisfactory proof will be found in Dr Manning's *Non-Euclidean Geometry*:

If two straight lines OP, OQ enclose an angle β, and if PQ is perpendicular to OQ at Q, then writing x, y for the lengths OQ, QP respectively,

for the elliptic hypothesis:

$$\tan \frac{y}{k} = \sin \frac{x}{k} \tan \beta;$$

and for the hyperbolic hypothesis:

$$\tanh \frac{y}{K} = \sinh \frac{x}{K} \tan \beta.$$

The parabolic metric is obtained by "making k (or K) infinite."

Comparing the equation of an equidistant

$$y = b$$

with the former pair of equations above, it at once appears that *for the elliptic and hyperbolic hypotheses, equidistants are not rectilinear.* In these two general cases, the equidistant is a curve, convex and concave, respectively, to its base.

It will also be convenient to add the formulae connecting

the sides a, b, c and the angles A, B, C of a triangle right-angled at A :

ELLIPTIC HYPOTHESIS	HYPERBOLIC HYPOTHESIS
$\cos \dfrac{a}{k} = \cos \dfrac{b}{k} \cos \dfrac{c}{k}$	$\cosh \dfrac{a}{K} = \cosh \dfrac{b}{K} \cosh \dfrac{c}{K}$
$\sin \dfrac{b}{k} = \sin \dfrac{a}{k} \sin B$	$\sinh \dfrac{b}{K} = \sinh \dfrac{a}{K} \sin B$
$\tan \dfrac{c}{k} = \tan \dfrac{a}{k} \cos B$	$\tanh \dfrac{c}{K} = \tanh \dfrac{a}{K} \cos B$
$\tan \dfrac{b}{k} = \sin \dfrac{c}{k} \tan B$	$\tanh \dfrac{b}{K} = \sinh \dfrac{c}{K} \tan B$
$\cos B = \cos \dfrac{b}{k} \sin C$	$\cos B = \cosh \dfrac{b}{K} \sin C$

These formulae contain the whole of the metric of the non-Euclidean geometries. Thus, if the angle B diminish to zero, the angle of parallelism C is determined by the last formula on the right:

$$1 = \cosh \frac{b}{K} \sin C.$$

It will be observed that the first formulae correspond to the Pythagorean Theorem (Euc. I. 47).

With these preliminaries, we may now commence the task of criticising Theories of Parallelism in the order of their appearance. Further developments of this brief Introduction will be found in the First Additional Note at the end of the volume.

EUCLID

Elements of Geometry, B.C. 300.

ɑ Venerated in Geometry more than Aristotle in Philosophy, the Elementist has enjoyed a fame excelled by none in the domain of pure knowledge. This well-merited fame has unfortunately hampered and impeded research into the Science of Space, and the more so on account of the strange transmutations of the text of the *Elements,* which have cloked the weaknesses of Euclid's method. This strange confusion as to first principles is displayed by the table below :

Editor	Date	Place	Postulates	Axioms
EUCLID	B.C. 300	Alexandria	5	5
Proclus	A.D. 450	Athens	5	5
Grynaeus	1533	Basle	3	11
Billingsley	1570	London	6	9
Gregory	1703	Oxford	3	12
Playfair	1795	Edinburgh	3	11
Peyrard	1814	Paris	6	9
Todhunter	1862	London	3	12

Referring to Dr Heath's magnificent edition of the *Elements* (Cambridge, 1908) for detailed information, we will reproduce here Euclid's first principles as he himself laid them down :

(A) *Necessary Concessions :*

(1) Let it be conceded that from every point to every point a straight line can be drawn ;

(2)   And a limited straight line can be produced continually in a straight line;

(3)   And for every centre and distance a circle can be described;

(4)   And all right angles are equal to each other;

(5)   And if a straight line falling on two straight lines make the angles within and towards the same parts less than two right angles, then the two straight lines being indefinitely produced meet towards the parts where are the angles less than two right angles.

(B)   *Universal Ideas:*

(1)   Equals to the same are also equal to each other;

(2)   And if to equals equals are added, the wholes are equal;

(3)   And if from equals equals are subtracted, the remainders are equal;

(4)   And things coinciding with each other are equal to each other;

(5)   And the whole is greater than the part.

How then were these employed by Euclid to uphold his view that in space as we know it there is through any given point a single duplex parallel to any given straight line?—On the one hand, he unconsciously assumed the infinitude of space; or rather, he was altogether unconscious of the validity of the hypothesis of the finite extent of space. It is practically impossible that he should ever have seriously entertained the idea that a straight line is a re-entrant line. Scarcely anyone had a rational glimpse of such a possibility before Riemann's day, that is, before the middle of the nineteenth century. Although the Third Postulate might be so understood as to bar out the elliptic hypothesis, it was not so devised (we must think) by Euclid himself. So the Elementist overlooked the possibility of there being no such thing at all as parallelism.

Thus on the other hand the possibility of double parallelism (hyperbolic hypothesis) was excluded by the Fifth Postulate, which is remarkably distinct in character from any other of the Postulates and Axioms. It ought not to be there, the student feels; still less ought it to be among the Axioms, for surely its occurrence *there* is one of the most ludicrous follies of which the human mind has ever had to plead guilty. Attempts at remedy have continually occupied the attention of the best Geometers of later times; and their curious failure quite to satisfy even themselves has hastened on the radical revision of the bases of Geometry.

The Parallel-Postulate (or Fifth Postulate, as we shall call it, avoiding the description of it as "Parallel-Axiom") was used by Euclid in his I. 29 in order to prove the converse of I. 27, 28. Let us restate these Theorems in their simplest forms, for purposes of criticism:

(I. 27, 28.) *If two straight lines AA', BB' have a common perpendicular MN, they never intersect.*

It is noteworthy that the Fifth Postulate supplies what is lacking here, in order to make MA, NB satisfy the strict definition of parallelism given above (page xv), which requires any straight line near MA within NMA to intersect NB. Euclid did not mention this; but gave a proof by means of his I. 16. Contrast Ptolemy's method below (page 6). But Euc. I. 16 is only universally valid in space of infinite extent. If space is of finite extent, and the straight line re-entrant (elliptic hypothesis), let ABC be a triangle so great that if D is the middle point of BC, AD is half the entire length of a straight line. Producing AD to A' such that $DA' = DA$, we shall find A' to be at A. Thus the congruence of the triangles BDA, CDA' shows that, if Ca is the prolongation of AC, the angle aCB or $A'CD$ is equal to the angle DBA or CBA. In this case, therefore, the exterior angle of the triangle would be equal to an interior opposite angle.

We conclude that the enunciation above would constitute a suitable Postulate for excluding the elliptic hypothesis; but it cannot be proved without assuming or postulating the infinitude of space. The companion enunciation now is:

1—2

(I. 29.) *If two straight lines AA', BB' do not intersect, they have any number of common perpendiculars like MN.*

For if N is any point in BB', and NM perpendicular thereto, then also NM is perpendicular to AA'; for, otherwise, the Parallel-Postulate would make either MA intersect NB or else MA' intersect NB', contrary to the enunciation.

Evidently, from the form in which they can be enunciated, Euc. I. 27, 28 and Euc. I. 29 are not completely converse. It is significant also that *if one single pair of straight lines were allowed to possess one single pair of common perpendiculars*, both the elliptic and hyperbolic hypotheses would be cancelled. In such a case the area/divergence constant would be infinite. The plane would then be of infinite size; and through any point there would be one duplex parallel to any straight line, as by (ii) page xiv.

In conclusion, the Fifth Postulate debars the hyperbolic hypothesis in an effective way, but it reads too much like a theorem and positively invites attempts at its proof.

POSIDONIUS

A lost work on Geometry, B.C. 80.

This Geometer was perhaps one of the earliest writers who defined parallels as equidistants. The assumption of the rectilinearity of equidistants disposes at once of the elliptic and hyperbolic hypotheses (see above, page xvii). " Posidonius says that parallel lines are such as neither converge nor diverge in one plane, but have all the perpendiculars drawn from points of one to the other equal. On the other hand such straight lines as make their perpendiculars continually greater or less will meet somewhere or other, because they converge towards each other " (Proclus, Friedlein's edition, page 176). The latter notion, only correct for the parabolic hypothesis, was re-affirmed as self-evident by Nasreddin (below, page 11).

GEMINUS

The Doctrine of Mathematics, B.C. 70.

Geminus was certainly a critic of first-rate ability. His scientific attitude is indicated in the often quoted words of his, recorded by Proclus : " We learned from the very pioneers of the Science never to allow our minds to resort to weak plausibilities for the advancement of geometrical reasoning"(Friedlein's edition, page 191). A theory of parallelism attributed to *Aganis* is found not in Proclus but in the *Commentary* of Anaritius (Curtze's edition, pages 66–73). So disappointing is this piece of work that it is a relief to find Dr Heath maintaining that Aganis was almost certainly not Geminus but some writer contemporary with Simplicius (A.D. 500). For instance, the following definition of equidistant lines is singularly lacking in precision : " These are such as lie in one surface, and when produced indefinitely have one space between them, and it is the least line between them." Assuming Euc. I. 1–26, Aganis would prove that : " If two straight lines are equidistant, the space between them is perpendicular to each of these lines." Here the rectilinearity of equidistants is definitely but tacitly assumed. Enunciated as a Postulate, this assumption is satisfactory, except that it assumes more than is necessary ; more (for instance) than the existence of a rectangle. Aganis' proof was :

" Let AA', BB' be two equidistant lines, and let MN be the space between them ; then the line MN is perpendicular to each of the lines AA', BB'. (Could a Greek mind think thus ?) For if the line MN were not perpendicular to each of the two lines AA', BB', the angles at the point M would not be right. Let therefore one of them AMN be an acute angle. Let me draw then from the point N a perpendicular Nm to the line AA', and let it fall on the side A. Then NM will be longer than Nm, from the proof of the tenth proposition. But this is to show that there is a line less than MN drawn between the lines AA', BB' ; which is contradictory and impossible. Therefore the line MN is perpendicular to each of the two lines AA', BB'."

The reference to Euc. I. 10 is very ingenious; the construction suggests the greater length of the oblique.

PTOLEMY

Tractate on Fifth Postulate, A.D. 150.

Ptolemy's interesting method of approaching the subject of Parallelism has been preserved in summary by Proclus (Friedlein's edition, pages 362–367). He assumed Euc. I. 1–26, including I. 16 which was unassailed until the latter half of last century. This application of Euc. I. 16 to unlimited areas banishes the elliptic hypothesis altogether. Although not perhaps quite so cogent in its original form, the first of Ptolemy's theorems to establish the Fifth Postulate was virtually as follows:

(1) If two straight lines AA' and BB' are crossed by a transversal MN so that the interior angles AMN, BNM on the same side of it are together equal to two right angles, then they cannot ever intersect.

For angles AMN, MNB' are equal. And if MA and NB were to meet at O, then by superposition of $AMNB$ upon $B'NMA'$, MA' and NB' would be found meeting at O' underneath O. But " two straight lines do not enclose a space "; and therefore it is impossible that AA' and BB' intersect at all.

Of course, O and O' may in their actual positions be the same point, and indeed are so in the (single) elliptic hypothesis. The postulate, not Euclidean but unobjectionable nevertheless, that two straight lines cannot intersect in two distinct points, does not prevent the elliptic hypothesis from being upheld and maintained. Methods being, if anything, more important than results, it may be observed that the above process by superposition is a fine artifice. The letter H provides a suitable figure. If the side-strokes meet above, they meet also below. If these points are somehow identical, space is *singly elliptic*; otherwise, *doubly elliptic*, an alternative only requiring mention.

Reference may be pardoned to the writer's *Story of Euclid*, despite its many faults, where a correct view-point (the greatest of all difficulties in these matters) is aimed at.

(2) Conversely, if AA' and BB' are parallel, and MN is a transversal, then the angles AMN, BNM are together equal to two right angles.

Ptolemy proved this thus: If the angles AMN, BNM are not together equal to two right angles, they are either greater, or else less. If they are together greater than two right angles, so also are the angles $A'MN$, $B'NM$, since "in no wise are MA and NB parallel more than MA' and NB'." But this would be impossible, because the four angles altogether make up four right angles; etc.

This proof presupposes one and only one parallel to BB' through M. It assumes what has been called the *duplex* character of parallelism, an unique feature of the parabolic hypothesis. This would have been better expressed explicitly as an alternative to the Fifth Postulate, after the manner of Proclus or Playfair. For in the hyperbolic hypothesis, when AA' and BB' are parallel in the strict sense, $A'A$ and $B'B$ are not parallel but only asecant (see below, page 43).

Two further theorems by Ptolemy in this connexion are given by Dr Heath in his *Elements* (pages 205–6, Vol. I.) in a note upon the Fifth Postulate, of which this volume must appear as an expansion.

PROCLUS

Commentary on the First Book of the Elements, A.D. 450.

The following passage from Proclus' *Commentary* might almost have been written by a nineteenth century Geometer like Lobachewski or J. Bolyai.

"It cannot be asserted unconditionally that straight lines produced from less than two right angles do not meet. It is of course obvious that some straight lines produced from less than two right angles do meet, but the (Euclidean) theory would require all such to intersect. But it might be urged that as the defect from two right angles increases, the straight lines continue asecant up to a certain magnitude of the defect, and for a greater magnitude than this they intersect."

Anyone who has been accustomed with M. Tannery to estimate Proclus' work at the level of industry rather than ingenuity should certainly compare the following very able treatment of a difficult problem with any other found in these pages. In the first place, Proclus adduced (Friedlein's edition, pages 371–373): *Aristotle's Axiom*: If from any point are drawn two straight lines enclosing an angle, then as they are indefinitely produced the distance between them exceeds every finite magnitude (*De Caelo*, Bk. I.). Although incapable of proof, this is well expressed, and excellently fitted to form a simple and useful Postulate. Sharply and clearly it excludes the elliptic hypothesis. If the elliptic hypothesis must needs be rejected at the outset, scarcely anything could be better.

In the second place, how did Proclus evade the hyperbolic hypothesis? He laid down a proposition, again clear, sharp, and sufficient. The only objection, and it is certainly a serious one, is that he attempted a proof, and did not (like his disciple Playfair) content himself with leaving it in the region of postulate. It was as follows:

Proclus' Proposition : If a straight line intersect one of two parallel straight lines, it will also intersect the other.

" For let AA' and BB' be parallels, and let aMa' cut AA' in M. I say that aMa' cuts BB'. For if the two straight lines MA, Ma are produced indefinitely from the point M, they have a distance greater than every magnitude, so that it is greater than the space between the parallels." Therefore Ma cuts BB'.

If instead of enunciating this proposition in the form of a postulate, the proof is to be made valid, some postulate must be laid down that the distance between AA' and BB' remains finite. The fact is doubtless that Proclus shared that conception of parallelism, as a single duplex relationship, which goes beyond the Euclidean definition. A suitable Postulate would be:

If two straight lines have a common perpendicular of finite length, the perpendiculars from points of one upon the other are all less than some assignable magnitude however great.

This is not the case in hyperbolic geometry. We know that the length of the perpendicular, at finite distance even, exceeds every finite magnitude, for by page xvii, the length

$$K \tanh^{-1} \left(\cosh \frac{x}{K} \tanh \frac{b}{K} \right)$$

becomes actually infinite for

$$x = K \cosh^{-1} \left(\coth \frac{b}{K} \right).$$

This is the very curious property of the hyperbolic plane, that a quadrilateral with three right angles may have two sides parallel, and the fourth vertex " at infinity." Thus the conception of the hyperbolic plane is fraught with difficulty, as is more readily confessed for the elliptic plane. Compare the criticism of Dodgson's figure below (page 52).

Proclus proved the Parallel-Postulate in the following manner:

" Let AA' and BB' be two straight lines, and let MN fall across them and make the angles AMN, BNM together less than two right angles....Let the angle aMA be made, equal to this defect from two right angles, and let aM be produced to a'. Then since MN falls across aa' and BB', and makes the interior angles aMN, BNM together equal to two right angles, the straight lines aa', BB' are parallel. But AA' cuts aa'. Therefore by the proposition above, AA' cuts BB' also. Therefore AA' and BB' intersect on the side where are the angles together less than two right angles."

An *obiter dictum* by Proclus (Friedlein's edition, page 374) that " Parallelism is similarity of position, if one may so say " illustrates admirably the Euclidean conception of parallelism; but the idea is vague, and useless for scientific purposes.

Modern geometrical research has discarded all such language. None the less, non-Euclidean Geometry has been stigmatised as a mere *façon de parler* (Dr Karagiannides, *Die Nichteuklidische Geometrie von Alterthum zur Gegenwart*, 1893), an unjust censure.

ANARITIUS

Commentary on the Elements, A.D. 900.

The *Commentary* of this Arab Geometer was translated into Latin by Gherard of Cremona about A.D. 1150, and this translation has been recently edited by Curtze (Leipzig, 1899). It is in this work that Aganis is so often mentioned (above, page 5). Apparently citing from the writings of Simplicius (A.D. 500), Anaritius reports the famous definition of a straight line, made more familiar in later days by Leibniz and Saccheri: *Linea recta est quaecumque super duas ipsius extremitates rotata non movetur de loco suo ad alium locum.* Anaritius did not treat independently of the Parallel-Postulate. On page 34 we read: "On this Simplicius said: This postulate is certainly not self-evident, and so it was necessary to prove it by lines."

GERBERT

Mathematical Works, A.D. 1000.

As would be expected of one who was not an Arab at this period, the works of Gerbert (afterwards Pope Sylvester II) contain no penetrative theory of parallelism. In his *Geometria* (IV. 10) he wrote: "Two straight lines distant from each other by the same space continually, and never meeting each other when indefinitely produced, are called *parallel*, that is, *equidistant*." Thus Gerbert assumed the rectilinearity of equidistants. At this time the results of Euclid, rather than his methods, were studied; and so were laid the foundations for

Savile's severe rebuke: *Homines stulti et perridiculi, quasi ullus unquam artifex suas edi voluerit conclusiones, nullis adjectis probationibus.*

NASREDDIN

Principles of Geometry, A.D. 1250.

Nasreddin's attempt to prove the Parallel-Postulate was explained by Wallis in a public lecture at Oxford on February 7th, 1651 (*Opera Mathematica*, Oxford, 1693; Vol. II. page 669). The Persian Geometer gave two Lemmas, the former of which he considered self-evident. These were substantially as follows:

(1) If AA' and BB' are two straight lines, and PQ is a perpendicular to BB' terminated by AA', and if these perpendiculars meet AA' at acute angles on the side of A, B; then the straight lines AA', BB' will approach each other towards A, B (so long as they do not intersect) and recede towards A', B'; and the perpendiculars will grow less on the side A, B, as far as the intersection of AA' and BB'; and greater on the side A', B'. And conversely.

"These two propositions are self-evident; and are so familiar to Geometers both ancient and modern that they are to be regarded as obvious."

This is scarcely axiomatic to-day. It is known that the perpendiculars may increase to a maximum (elliptic hypothesis), or decrease to a minimum (hyperbolic hypothesis), according to formulae containing circular or hyperbolic functions (see above, page xvii). It is true that the angles change their character in accordance with the Lemma. But the possibility of a maximum or minimum perpendicular intervening between AB and $A'B'$ vitiates the proof of the second Lemma. If this possibility were expressly negated, then the first Lemma would make an efficient substitute for the Parallel-Postulate.

(2) If AB, $A'B'$ are equal perpendiculars to BB', then the angles at A and A' are right.

For if the angle $A'AB$ is not right, suppose it (for instance) acute. Then by (1) AA' approaches BB' towards A', B'; and therefore $A'B'$ is of lesser length than AB, contrary to the supposition.

Having thus secured the existence of a rectangle, Nasreddin proved Euc. I. 32 and the Fifth Postulate. See Dr Heath's *Elements* (Vol. I. page 209).

BILLINGSLEY

The Elements of Geometrie, A.D. 1570.

Afterwards Lord Mayor of London, Sir Henry Billingsley edited the first printed edition of Euclid's *Elements* in English. He was familiar with Campanus' translation from Arabic into Latin, but his notes on I. 16, 28 were derived from Proclus. Under the heading : " Peticions or requestes," we read :

" 5. When a right line falling upon two right lines, doth make on one and the selfe same syde, the two inwarde angles lesse then two right angles, then shal these two right lines beyng produced at length concurre on that part, in which are the two angles lesse then two right angles.

...For the partes of the lines towardes (the one side) are more inclined the one to the other, then the partes of the lines towardes (the other side) are...."

Billingsley did not separate out what-is-defined from what-is-proved sufficiently. His 35th Definition ran :

" Parallel or equidistant right lines are such ; which being in one and the selfe same superficies, and produced infinitely on both sydes, do never in any part concurre."

But as Dr Henrici well says : "A good definition must state as many properties as are sufficient to decide whether a thing belongs to a class or not, but not more than are necessary for this purpose" (*Congruent Figures*, London, 1891, page 33).

CLAVIUS

Euclidis Elementorum Libri xv., Rome, 1574.

Clavius followed Proclus in revising the theory of Parallelism, and endeavoured to prove the Aristotelian Axiom that the distance between two intersecting straight lines increases beyond limit. Thus:

Let OMM' and ONN' be two intersecting straight lines, and let MN, $M'N'$ be perpendiculars upon ONN'. If possible, let MN and $M'N'$ be of equal length. Take along $N'NO$ the length $N'O'$ equal to NO. Then the triangles MNO, $M'N'O'$ are congruent. Therefore the angles MON, $M'O'N'$ are equal, contrary to Euc. I. 16.

Or again, if possible, let MN exceed $M'N'$ in length, although O, N, N' are in this order. Take in that case a length $N'm'$ along $N'M'$ equal to NM. Then as before the angles $m'O'N'$ and MON are equal. That is, if $m'O'$ meets OMM' in m, the angles mON, $mO'N'$ are equal, contrary to Euc. I. 16.

This is excellently arranged; but it suggests only what is already known, that Euc. I. 16 is universally valid only in an infinite space. Euclid's 16th proposition and Aristotle's axiom contain the same assumption, the same principle, namely, that the plane is of infinite size. Such three statements are equivalent; and any one of them is sufficient to free Geometry from the elliptic hypothesis.

Clavius also laboured to make evident from general considerations (which is often an unprofitable task in Geometry) that equidistants are rectilinear. "For if all the points of the line AA' are equally distant from the straight line BB', its points will be disposed evenly (*ex aequo*),"—not crookedly, therefore rectilinearly. But the straight line is not the only uniform line. For instance, as Clavius himself remarked, the equidistant to a circle is a circle.

OLIVER

De Rectarum Linearum Parallelismo, Cambridge, 1604.

Thomas Oliver, Physician, of Bury, gave two somewhat weak attempts at the proof of the Fifth Postulate. These were on the following lines:

First Method: To prove that if MN is a perpendicular to BB', and of unvarying length, then NM is always perpendicular to " the right line described by the other extremity," M; and if NM is always perpendicular to AA', then N describes BB' in like manner.

For let MN, AB be positions of the perpendicular, then MAB is to be proved a right angle. Take NB' equal to NB along BN, and let $A'B'$ be the position of the perpendicular at B'. Then the triangle ABN can be superposed upon the triangle $A'B'N$, and is congruent thereto. Hence $AN, A'N$ are equal; and angles ANM, $A'NM$ are equal. Hence the triangles $ANM, A'NM$ are congruent. And so MN is perpendicular to AA'—if (we must add) AMA' is one straight line.

Second Method: If AM and BN are both perpendicular to MN, then any perpendicular from a point A of AM upon BN is equal in length to MN, and is perpendicular to MA.

For let NM be moved so as to lie along BA, then shall M fall upon A. Otherwise, let NM assume the position Ba. Produce BN to B', making NB' equal in length to NB; and let MN move along NB' into the position $a'B'$ perpendicular to NB' at B'. Join Na, Na'. Then the triangles $NBa, NB'a'$ are superposable, and so congruent. Hence the lengths Na, Na' are equal; and the angles MNa, MNa' are seen to be equal. Thus the triangles MNa, MNa' are superposable, and congruent. Therefore the angles NMa, NMa' are equal, and hence are right angles; so that the angles AMN, aMN are equal, which is impossible.

It is assumed that aMa' is one straight line, which is another working of the assumption that equidistants are rectilinear.

SAVILE

Praelectiones XIII. *in Principia Euclidis Elementorum,*
Oxford, 1621.

Sir Henry Savile founded Chairs of Geometry and Astronomy
at Oxford. He commended two problems for consideration by
the professor of Geometry. One of these was the Euclidean
theory of parallelism; the other, the Euclidean theory of proportion. He expressed his dissatisfaction in epigrammatic
form: *In pulcherrimo Geometriae corpore duo sunt naevi,
duae labes.* These "blots" were the Fifth Postulate, and the
Fifth Definition of Book VI. (the latter not really Euclid's; see
Dr Heath's *Elements, ad locum*). Savile died the year after his
lectures were published; and a generation elapsed before John
Wallis brought his talents to bear upon the two difficulties.

TACQUET

Elementa Geometriae Planae et Solidae, Amsterdam, 1654.

The illustrious Whiston stated in his *Memoirs* that "it was
the accidental purchase of Tacquet's own Euclid at an auction
which occasioned his first application to the Mathematics,
wherein Tacquet was a very clear writer."

Tacquet defined parallels to be equidistants, giving as his
reason for so doing: *Euclidaea definitio parallelismi naturam
non satis explicat.* But he went further, and inserted as
Axioms:

(11) Parallel lines have a common perpendicular,

(12) Two perpendiculars cut off equal segments from each
of two parallels.

Concerning these he remarked that "their truth is immediately apparent from the definition of parallelism." Nevertheless
he condemned the Parallel-Postulate, at that time often reckoned
Eleventh Axiom: *non axioma sed theorema.* His proof of it

was neither very elegant nor very cogent.   And still further, he posited yet another " axiom," that two parallels to the same straight line do not intersect.   However clear a writer, therefore, Tacquet would not be considered convincing by a modern critic.

HOBBES

De Corpore, 1655 : *et caetera.*

" There is in Euclid a definition of strait-lined parallels; but I do not find that parallels in general are anywhere defined; and therefore for an universal definition of them, I say that any two lines whatsoever, strait or crooked, as also any two superficies, are *parallel*, when two equal strait lines, wheresoever they fall upon them make equal angles with each of them.   From which definition it follows; first, that any two strait lines, not inclined opposite ways, falling upon two other strait lines, which are parallel, and intercepting equal parts in both of them, are themselves also equal and parallel" (*De Corpore*, c. 14, § 12).

Hobbes' definition of parallelism contains too much, when applied to straight lines.   A rectilinear parallel to a straight line given should be determinate by a single characteristic (*e.g.* a single act of construction, as would be the case if Euc. I. 31 were made to furnish a definition).   When thus defined, its other properties should be then proved.   Otherwise, something has been defined of which the existence is not immediately clear.   It is wrong to assume two straight lines AA' and BB' such that if a transversal MN meet them in M and N, then if $M'N'$ is any other transversal equal to MN in length, the angle $M'N'B'$ can always be equal to the angle MNB'.   The commonsense philosopher should not veil such assumptions under definitions.

Hobbes failed to disentangle the knots in the prevalent scheme of Geometry.   He justly urged against Euclid's definition: "How shall a man know that there be strait lines which shall never meet though both ways infinitely produced?" (*Collected Works*, Vol. 7, page 206). But the challenge applies still more forcibly to his own definition given above, which Hobbes had the hardihood to reproduce in this place: "Parallels are those lines and superficies between which every line drawn in any angle is equal to any other line drawn in the same angle the same way." How shall a man know that there be such straight lines or plane surfaces?

WALLIS

Demonstratio Postulati Quinti Euclidis, 1663.

Of different character from the preceding is the cautious, penetrative work of this Savilian Professor, delivered as a public lecture at Oxford on the evening of July 11th, 1663, and published in his *Collected Works* (Oxford, 1693, Vol. 2, pages 674–678).

"It is known," he began, "that some of the ancient geometers, as well as the modern, have censured Euclid for having postulated, as a concession required without demonstration, the *Fifth Postulate*, or (as others say) the *Eleventh Axiom*, or, with the enumeration of Clavius, the *Thirteenth Axiom*... But those who discover this fault in Euclid do themselves very often (at least, as far as I have examined them) make other assumptions in place of it, and these appear to me no easier to allow than what Euclid postulates... Since nevertheless I observe that so many have attempted a proof, as if they esteemed it necessary, I have thought good to add my own effort, and to endeavour to bring forward a proof that may be less open to objection than theirs."

Wallis first laid down seven Lemmas of a simple and unexceptionable character; but the eighth contained something of radical significance for the Theory of Parallelism.

"VIII. At this stage, presupposing a knowledge of the nature of ratio and the definition of similar figures, I assume as an universal idea: *To any given figure whatever, another figure, similar and of any size, is possible.* Because continuous quantities are capable both of illimitable division and illimitable increase, this seems to result from the very nature of quantity; namely, that a figure can be continuously diminished or increased illimitably, the form of the figure being retained."

Although Wallis' argument is insufficient, this Principle of Similitude might make a suitable substitute for Euclid's Fifth, postulate for postulate; and moreover it has the advantage of negating the elliptic hypothesis. Wallis however stated more than is really necessary for a proper postulate. If a single pair of triangles can be found in a plane, of different areas but of equal angle-sums, then the geometry of that plane is Euclidean. For let Δ, Δ' be the areas, and δ the common divergence, then as on page xiii above, $\Delta = A \cdot \delta$, $\Delta' = A \cdot \delta$, where A is a constant over the plane. But $\Delta \neq \Delta'$; and therefore δ must be zero, and A infinite; and the geometry of the plane is parabolic.

Wallis' proof of the Fifth Postulate was effected thus: Let MA, NB be two straight lines making with MN the angles AMN, BNM together less than two right angles. Suppose the angle AMN to slide along MN until M reaches N. Then because the angle AMN is less than the supplement of the angle BNM, AM in its final position will be outside BNM. Therefore at some position of MA before M reaches N, say ma, MA will intersect NB, say at p. Now by the principle of similitude, it is possible to draw on MN a triangle similar to the triangle mNp. Therefore corresponding to the point p there exists a point P wherein MA and NB intersect. Q.E.D.

LEIBNIZ

Characteristica Geometrica, 1679; *In Euclidis* ΠΡΩΤΑ; etc.

Leibniz's geometrical tracts have been gathered together in the first volume of his collected mathematical writings (Gerhardt's edition, Halle, 1858). Like his contemporary and rival Newton, Leibniz was a thorough-going Euclidean at heart. His criticisms are acute and his suggestions valuable. A plane surface results when a solid is cut in two so that the surfaces of section are exactly similar, even when reversed. A straight line is obtained by cutting a plane so that the lines of division are superposable in any position, including the reversed. On the Euclidean definition of parallelism Leibniz wrote: "This definition seems rather to describe parallels by means of a more remote property than that which they most evidently display; and one might doubt whether the relationship exists, or whether all straight lines in the plane do not ultimately intersect each other" (page 200). This is a logical premonition of the elliptic hypothesis. Leibniz gave an attempt at a demonstration of the existence of rectangles; but the times were not yet ripe.

DA BITONTO

Euclide Restituto, 1680.

Like Leibniz, this Italian geometer would prefer a positive definition of parallelism. To justify his own definition of parallels as equidistants, he laid down fifteen or more propositions, analysed and discussed by Camerer in the edition of Euclid only surpassed by Dr Heath's new work. Da Bitonto's fifth proposition was: The perpendiculars let fall from points of any curve upon any straight line cannot all be equal. This would imply the rectilinearity of equidistants; but the proof does not hold good for any straight line whatever.

SACCHERI

Euclides ab omni naevo Vindicatus, Milan, 1733.

Saccheri's work was forgotten until about twenty years ago. The remarks of Dr Stäckel in this connexion are well worth repeating at considerable length, from the preface to that scholarly and compact volume in which the reader will find a full recension of the Jesuit professor's apology for Euclid (Engel and Stäckel, *Die Theorie der Parallel-linien von Euklid bis auf Gauss*, Leipzig, 1895, pages 41–136).

" Quite thirty years have elapsed since by the publication of Riemann's Inaugural Dissertation, and by the appearance of Helmholtz's Memoir (on the Hypotheses at the basis of Geometry), the *space-problem* and the associated *parallel-question* became matters of general and abiding interest. About the same time it became known that Gauss had realised long ago the possibility and validity of a geometry independent of the Parallel-Axiom, and the rescue from oblivion of the writings of Lobachewski and J. Bolyai was effected, wherein this (hyperbolic) geometry was systematically developed. Gauss, Lobachewski and J. Bolyai were now the putative originators of non-Euclidean Geometry, of which the further development and firmer establishment were the work of Riemann and Helmholtz. Then a certain stir was created in 1889 when Beltrami pointed out that as early as 1733 an Italian Jesuit, Gerolamo Saccheri, in an attempt to prove Euclid's Fifth Postulate, had been led to a series of propositions hitherto ascribed to Lobachewski and J. Bolyai.... Then the idea occurred to me whether possibly Saccheri's *Euclides ab omni naevo Vindicatus* might not prove to be a link in the chain of an historical development, so that the fundamental principle of continuity might perhaps prevail in the evolution of non-Euclidean Geometry.... In the first yearly issue (of the *Magazin für die reine und angewandte Mathematik*) a memoir on the theory of parallels by Johann Heinrich Lambert excited my attention, and a fuller examination led to the startling conclusion that Lambert must be considered a hitherto disregarded forerunner of Gauss, Lobachewski and J. Bolyai."

Saccheri protested against the procedure of early Geometers who "assume, not without great violence to strict logic, that parallel lines are equally distant from each other, as though that were given *a priori*, and then pass on to the proofs of the other theorems connected therewith" (page 46).

It would be a lengthy task to make a detailed discussion of the *Euclides Vindicatus*. Saccheri promises that he will apply Euc. I. 16, 17 only to triangles limited in every direction, yet has no suspicion about the infinitude of space. He employs Euc. I. 1–15, 18–26 with entire freedom. The hyperbolic hypothesis survives the elliptic for some pages. We may sketch a few of his earlier propositions:

(1) If two equal straight lines $AB, A'B'$ make equal angles with any straight line BB' on the same side, the angles of the quadrilateral at A and A' are equal. This might be proved by superposition; but Saccheri employs Euc. I. 4, 8 mediately.

(2) If the sides AA', BB' of such a quadrilateral are bisected in M, N, then MN is perpendicular to AA' and BB'. This follows from (1) by Euc. I. 4, 8. A simple and direct proof by superposition would suffice.

(3) *If two equal straight lines $AB, A'B'$ are perpendicular to BB', the side AA' of the quadrilateral is equal to, or less than, or greater than, the opposite side BB', according as the equal angles at A, A' are right, or obtuse, or acute, respectively.*

This highly important General Theorem is proved in the following way:

CASE I. *When the equal angles at A, A' are right.*

For AA' is not greater than BB'; since if it were so, a length $A'a$ might be taken along $A'A$ equal to $B'B$. Then angles $B'Ba, BaA'$ would be equal (Prop. 1). But angle $B'Ba$ is less than $B'BA$; and angle BaA' is greater than BAA'

(Euc. I. 16); so that angle $B'Ba$ is less than BaA'. Nor is AA' less than BB', in like manner. And so AA' is equal to BB'.

CASE II.   *When the equal angles at A, A' are obtuse.*

Bisect AA', BB' in M, N; then MN is perpendicular to both AA' and BB'. Now AM is not equal to BN; for if so, angles MAB, NBA would be equal; and they are not. Moreover AM is not greater than BN. For if so, take along MA a length Ma equal to NB. Then angles MaB, NBa are equal (Prop. 1). But angle NBa is less than a right angle; and angle MaB is greater than aAB (Euc. I. 16), which is obtuse, so that angle MaB is decidedly greater than a right angle. [Consideration of the figure will show that Euc. I. 16 is applicable even in this case of the elliptic hypothesis, because the join of B to the middle point of Aa is less than BP, P being the intersection of this join with NM; and BP is less than BO, O being the intersection of BA and NM. That is, BP is less than half the complete length of a straight line ; because, if BP were equal to BO, angle BON would be right, and B coincide with B'; and if BP were greater than BO, angle BON would be obtuse, and BB' overlap itself.] Thus angle MaB exceeds NBa. Therefore AM cannot be greater than BN. And AM is not equal to BN. Hence AM is less than BN.

CASE III.   *When the equal angles at A, A' are acute.*

The proof is similar to that of Case II.

These three Cases Saccheri termed the Hypotheses of the Right Angle, of the Obtuse Angle, and of the Acute Angle, respectively.   They were afterwards called the Parabolic, Elliptic, and Hyperbolic Hypotheses by Dr Klein (see below, page 50).

(5 (6), (7)   If the Hypothesis of the Right, the Obtuse, or the Acute Angle holds good for one quadrilateral of the kind under consideration, it holds good for every such quadrilateral throughout the entire plane.

The somewhat lengthy proofs make repeated use of Euc. I. 16, 17 (pages 54–58).

"(14) The Hypothesis of the Obtuse Angle is completely false, because self-contradictory."

The second of Saccheri's proofs ran as follows:

"Since we have proved, with the Hypothesis of the Obtuse Angle, that the two acute angles of a triangle ABC, right-angled at B, are together greater than a right angle, it is evident that an acute angle BAD can be assumed (on the outer side of BA) to make with them two right angles. Then the straight line AD, by the foregoing Proposition (asserting the Parallel-Postulate) for the Hypothesis of the Obtuse Angle, ultimately meets CB. This however clearly contradicts Euc. I. 17," because if AD meets CB in E, then the triangle EAC has its angles at A and C together equal to two right angles. Saccheri failed to observe the possible re-entrance of straight lines into themselves, a main feature of the elliptic hypothesis of space.

It may be noted that Mansion has given the name *Saccheri's Theorem* to the proposition that in the hyperbolic plane two straight lines which do not intersect have in general a common perpendicular. The exceptional case is when they are not merely asecant but parallel (*Mathesis*, Vol. 16 Supplt, 1896). We may also observe in connexion with Saccheri's work that Clairaut in 1741 enunciated an alternative to the Parallel-Postulate in the simple form, that a rectangle exists.

SIMSON

Euclidis elementorum libri priores sex... Glasgow, 1756.

The famous Robert Simson offered a proof of the "Eleventh Axiom" by a method involving a new Axiom, in the following manner:

Definition 1. The distance of a point from a straight line is the perpendicular from the point upon the straight line.

Definition 2. A straight line is said to approach towards, or recede from, another straight line according as the distances of points of the former from the latter decrease or increase. Two straight lines are equidistant, if points of the one preserve the same distance from the other.

Axiom : A straight line cannot approach towards, and then recede from, a straight line without cutting it; nor can a straight line approach towards, then be equidistant to, and then recede from, a straight line ; for a straight line preserves always the same direction.

Simson appealed to common sense and common experience, a proper course for educational purposes. Scientifically, it would have been better to postulate this property of straight lines which is peculiar to the parabolic hypothesis; and also to refrain from introducing the idea of direction for support. The suggestion of Peletarius (1557) that even Axioms themselves be reckoned as Definitions (defining the relations spoken of in them) has been generally accepted to-day for scientific purposes. The tendency of the educationalist as such is in the opposite direction, of making as much as possible present an axiomatic appearance to the inexperienced eye of the child.

Simson's first proposition, proved by means of his axiom, was :

If two equal straight lines AB, $A'B'$ are perpendicular to any straight line BB', and if from any point M of the join AA' a perpendicular MN is let fall upon BB', then AB and MN and $A'B'$ are equal to one another in length.

This proposition puts an Euclidean impress upon the geometry of the plane.

LAMBERT

Die Theorie der Parallel-linien, 1766.

If two explorers, strangers to each other, enter an unknown land beyond the mountains by the same pass, they may quite possibly be found to have chosen the same route for some distance into the interior; and so considerable likeness exists

between the work of Clavius, Lambert and J. Bolyai and the
earlier work of Nasreddin, Saccheri and Lobachewski. The
similarity between Saccheri's treatise and Lambert's memoir is
easily seen in the pages of Engel and Stäckel's volume. Lambert
employed for his fundamental figure a quadrilateral with three
right angles, which is the half of one of Saccheri's isosceles
quadrilaterals. He stated expressly that the opposite sides of
his quadrilateral did not meet, a fatal blow to the elliptic
hypothesis. Thus, for instance, in § 33 he wrote (with reference
to a standard quadrilateral $ABB'A'$, wherein three of the angles
at A, B and B' are right angles), "the fact that AA' and BB'
do not intersect leaves it unsettled whether the distances AB
and $A'B'$ are always equal or greater or less" (page 178).

In § 39 Lambert considered a figure in which BN, NB' are
equal distances along BB'; AB, MN, $A'B'$ perpendiculars to
BNB'; and AMA' perpendicular to NM at M. He then
wrote :

" The question now arises about the angle at A ; and therefore we are bound to formulate three Hypotheses. For it may
be that

$$\text{the angle } MAB \text{ is} \begin{cases} \text{equal to } 90°, & \text{(i)} \\ \text{or greater than } 90°, & \text{(ii)} \\ \text{or less than } 90°. & \text{(iii)} \end{cases}$$

These three Hypotheses I will adopt in order, and educe their
consequences."

These are again the parabolic, elliptic and hyperbolic
hypotheses of Dr Klein. The elliptic hypothesis (ii) soon
dropped out of Lambert's hands, owing to his extension to the
entire (infinite) plane of results into which Euc. I. 16 enters.
But the hyperbolic hypothesis (iii) was successfully worked out
to conclusions implying an absolute standard of length. On
this Lambert remarked (§§ 80, 81):

" This consequence possesses a charm which makes one
desire that the Third Hypothesis be indeed true !

" Yet on the whole I would not wish it true, notwithstand-
ing this advantage (of an absolute standard of length), since
innumerable difficulties would be involved therewith. Our

trigonometrical tables would become immeasurably vast (compare pages xviii and 57, above and below); the similitude and proportionality of geometrical figures would wholly disappear, so that no figure can be represented except in its actual size; astronomy would be harassed (see our Second Additional Note); etc.

" Still these are *argumenta ab amore et invidiâ ducta*, which must be banished from Geometry as from every science.

" I revert accordingly to the Third Hypothesis. In this hypothesis, as already seen, not only is the sum of the three angles of every triangle less than 180°; but this difference from 180° increases directly with the area of the triangle; that is to say, if of two triangles one has a greater area than the other, then in the first the sum of the three angles is less than in the second."

Then in § 82 Lambert surmised that the area of a triangle is actually proportional to the difference between its angle-sum and two right angles. This has been called *Lambert's Theorem* by Mansion (*Mathesis*, Supplt 1896, *Premiers Principes de la Metagéométrie*).

BERTRAND

Développement Nouveau de la Partie Élémentaire des Mathématiques, Geneva, 1778.

We furnish here a few all too brief extracts from the elegant and perspicuous disquisitions of this Swiss Geometer.

" Geometry, like every other science, has its roots in ideas common to all. From this fount of ideas the first originators derived those principles and germs of knowledge which they bestowed upon mankind. Hence it appears that in every science two parts can be distinguished; the first, consisting of the assemblage of principles or primitive conceptions from which the science proceeds; and a second, comprising the development of the consequences of the principles. In respect of these principles as they exist in every mind, science would seem to encounter no resistance or difficulty. Yet the choice that has to be made of first principles, the degree of simplicity and elegance to which they have to be reduced, and the necessity of enunciating them in precise terms, capable of clear comprehension,—all this is very difficult."

Bertrand now adduced the practical illustration of a Hunter, having shot a deer, measuring the length of his shot in bowlengths, and meditating upon the sense of direction exercised when he aimed the fatal arrow. He then proceeded with much eloquence: "The spectacle of the universe displays before our eyes an immense space. In this immensity bodies exist and change continually their shape, size and position; and meanwhile space itself, invariable in all its parts, remains like a sea always calm, in everlasting repose. So the idea we form of space is that it is infinite and limitless; homogeneous and like itself at every time and in every place. Space is without bounds, for any we might assign to it would be contained in it, and therefore would not bound it. Space is homogeneous, in that the portion of space occupied by a body in one plane would not differ from that which would be occupied by it elsewhere."

Division of space into two halves identical in all but position gives the plane surface; and division of the plane similarly gives the straight line (so also Leibniz, above, page 19).

So far, so good. But the elliptic hypothesis escapes from the Hunter's grasp in his seventh effort of thought, as from Ptolemy's many centuries before.

"*Proposition* 7. Two straight lines AMA', BMB' traced on the same plane, and making with a third MN the interior angles AMN, BNM of which the sum is equal to two right angles, cannot intersect."

For $AMNB$ can be superposed upon $B'NMA'$. "Hence it will follow that the straight lines AA', BB' will intersect in two points, or will not intersect at all. But the first is impossible, therefore the second is true."

This is incisive; but as remarked above (page 6) these presumably very distant points may be one and the same point.

The Hunter's thoughts are supposed to turn next to an eighth Proposition, equivalent to the following: The plane contains an infinite number of strips such as are formed by two perpendiculars MA, NB to a limited straight line MN on the same side of it. For if MN is produced to P, and NP is equal to MN, and PC drawn perpendicular to NP, then the strip $AMNB$ can be superposed upon the strip $BNPC$. And space being infinite by the preceding Proposition, this process, repeated infinitely often, furnishes an infinite number of strips, congruent to $AMNB$, over half of the infinite plane.

Then the Hunter elaborates one of the finest proofs of the Parallel-Postulate of which we have knowledge, after this manner:

Let MH be drawn within the strip $AMNB$; then MH meets NB. For the area included within the angle AMH is a *finite* fraction of the area of the entire plane; in fact, the same fraction that the angle AMH is for a denominator of four right angles. Whereas the area of the strip $AMNB$ has been seen to be only an *infinitesimal* fraction of the whole plane; in fact, the same fraction that the length MN is for an infinite denominator (the whole length of a straight line). Hence the angle AMH cannot be contained within the strip $AMNB$. Therefore it must overlap. Therefore MH must intersect and cross NB.

This is exceedingly forcible, indeed almost overwhelming. It seems to pierce the heart of the hyperbolic hypothesis, like a swift arrow from a sure bow. Let us see whether any light is shed upon it by our results for the hyperbolic hypothesis on page xvii above. The area of the angle AMH is a certain definite fraction of the area of the infinite plane. Take then a circle of any assigned radius R however large, its centre being M. The area of this circle is

$$2\pi K \int_0^R \sinh \frac{x}{K}\,dx = 2\pi K^2 \left(\cosh \frac{R}{K} - 1 \right).$$

When R becomes indefinitely great, even compared with the space-constant K, the value of this expression is of the order of magnitude $\pi K^2 e^{\frac{R}{K}}$. Thus if the angle AMH is β in circular measure, the area of the sector AMH is not very different from

$$\frac{\beta}{2} K^2 e^{\frac{R}{K}}.$$

Now let us consider the area of the strip $AMNB$, and write b for the length MN, then by considering a very great number of very narrow strips all of length R, we have for the area required

$$b \int_0^R \cosh \frac{x}{K}\, dx = bK \sinh \frac{R}{K},$$

which is not very different from $\frac{b}{2} K e^{\frac{R}{K}}$, the further boundary of the strip being an equidistant on MN of height R.

Thus the ratio of the areas of sector and strip, computed thus, is practically $\frac{\beta}{b} K$, which is always finite; and indeed may be made as small as desired by choosing the angle β small enough.

There may be observed an inconsistency in the areas of the hyperbolic plane computed by means of an infinite number of sectors and an infinite number of strips. A circle of very great radius R has area $\pi K^2 e^{\frac{R}{K}}$ approximately. But a double strip of length $2R$ has an area of about $bK e^{\frac{R}{K}}$. And as the number of strips is certainly infinite, the area of the plane reckoned in strips infinitely exceeds the area of the plane reckoned in sectors. The reason is this. The space between a circle of great diameter $2R$ and the equilateral circumscribing quadrilateral of medial dimensions $2R$, is ultimately infinite compared with the area of the circle, in the hyperbolic hypothesis. There is a like point to be raised in criticism of Dodgson's figure (below, page 52).

None the less, the above piece of rigorous analysis is very different from that simple, convincing objection which one would wish to raise. The only possible elementary criticism appears to be that more is assumed about the infinite regions of the plane than we can really know or conceive. Probably the experts will consider the argument, on this or other grounds, one of the most plausible and fallacious of sophisms.

For the hyperbolic hypothesis, the rectangular strip widens out ultimately at the same rate as a circular sector; and our mental picture of such infinitely distant regions is not legitimate unless drawing to scale (Wallis' principle) is a legitimate and indeed possible procedure. If there is no court of appeal from the verdict of "commonsense," Bertrand's argument stands, and Euclid's geometry prevails.

PLAYFAIR

Elements of Geometry, Edinburgh, 1795.

John Playfair was a typical expositor of Euclidean Geometry. What has become generally known as Playfair's Axiom is only a slightly varied form of Proclus' Proposition (above, page 8). Playfair wrote:

"A new Axiom is introduced in the room of the 12th, for the purpose of demonstrating more easily some of the properties of parallel lines."

This new Axiom, assigned the 11th place, was couched in the familiar terms:

"Two straight lines which intersect one another, cannot be both parallel to the same straight line."

As will be seen by a comparison with Lobachewski's position (below, page 43), this prevents the hyperbolic hypothesis; and the elliptic hypothesis would probably have been thought by Playfair to be sufficiently frustrated by the corollary to his definition of the straight line, that two straight lines cannot enclose a space.

Of this Axiom of Playfair's, Cayley said : " My own view is that Euclid's Twelfth Axiom in Playfair's form of it, does not need demonstration, but is part of our notion of space, of the physical space of our experience, which is the representation lying at the bottom of all external experience " (*Presidential Address to the British Association*, 1883). Dr Russell cites and criticises this interesting confession in his admirable *Foundations of Geometry* (Cambridge, 1899, page 41).

LAPLACE

Exposition du Système du Monde, Paris, 1796.

This great Analyst expressed his views to a certain extent, in connexion with the Law of Universal Gravitation (Harte's translation, Dublin, 1830, page 321).

"The law of attraction, inversely as the square of the distance, is that of emanations which proceed from a centre... One of its remarkable properties is, that if the dimensions of all the bodies in the universe, their mutual distances and velocities, increase or diminish proportionally, they describe curves entirely similar to those which they at present describe ; so that if the universe be successively reduced to the smallest imaginable space, it will always present the same appearance to all observers... The simplicity of the laws of nature therefore only permits us to observe the relative dimensions of space."

On the other hand, Gauss (below, page 34) remarked the possibility of objects possessing absolute dimensions ; and the analysis of celestial mechanics becomes much more intricate if the law of the inverse square has to be abandoned or assigned a subordinate place. For the elliptic and hyperbolic hypotheses, the area of a sphere of radius r is

$$4k^2 \sin^2 \frac{r}{k} \quad \text{and} \quad 4K^2 \sinh^2 \frac{r}{K}$$

respectively. Thus the law of intensity of radiation issuing uniformly from a point-source would for the three hypotheses be expressed by the factors

$$\operatorname{cosec}^2\frac{r}{k}, \quad r^{-2}, \quad \operatorname{cosech}^2\frac{r}{K}.$$

The application of these extended laws to planetary motion is the task undertaken in the Second Additional Note to this volume (page 62).

The translator's note (page 536) may be reproduced here:

"The endeavours of Geometers to demonstrate Euclid's Twelfth Axiom about parallel lines have been hitherto unsuccessful. However no person questions the truth of this Axiom, or of the Theorems which Euclid has deduced from it. The perception of extension contains therefore a peculiar property which is self-evident, without which we could not rigorously establish the doctrine of parallels. The notion of a limited extension (for example, of a circle) does not involve anything that depends on its absolute magnitude; but if we conceive its radius to be diminished, we are forced to diminish in the same proportion its circumference, and the sides of all the inscribed figures. This proportionality was, according to Laplace, much more obvious than that of Euclid. It is curious to observe that agreeably to what is stated on page 322, this Axiom is pointed out in the results of universal gravitation."

Certainly the utterances of great minds are always deserving of careful attention, and repay it.

GAUSS

Letters and Reviews, 1799–1846.

For nearly fifty years the mind of Gauss was repeatedly engaged upon the hyperbolic hypothesis, styled by him *non-Euclidean Geometry.* His occasional writings, collected by Engel and Stäckel, are humanly interesting. His influence was exerted upon the elder Bolyai, and so indirectly upon the brilliant son, Johann Bolyai. In a letter to the father towards the close of the year 1799, Gauss wrote:

" I have arrived at much which most people would regard as proved, but it is in my eyes good for nothing in this respect. For example, if it could be proved that a rectilinear triangle is possible, of area exceeding any assigned area, I should be in a position to prove rigorously the whole of (Euclidean) geometry. Now most people would regard this as axiomatic, but I do not. It would be quite possible that however distant from each other the vertices of the triangle were assumed to lie in space, the area should still be less than an assignable limit. I have more propositions of a similar character, but in none of them do I find anything really satisfying."

In fact, the maximum area of a triangle formed by three straight lines for the hyperbolic hypothesis would be

$$K^2(\pi - A - B - C),$$

wherein $A = B = C = 0$, that is, πK^2, which though probably large is strictly limited. The sides of the triangle would be parallel in pairs, and the vertices " at infinity."

Thus Gauss seems to have worked out several fundamental theorems of hyperbolic geometry but not so completely as to feel ready to publish them. His letter to Taurinus, a facsimile of which forms the frontispiece to *Parallel-linien von Euklid bis auf Gauss*, reads as follows :

" I have read not without pleasure your kind letter of October 30th with the small sketch enclosed, the more so because I have been accustomed to discover scarcely any trace of pure geometrical spirit among the majority of people who make the new attempts on the so-called Theory of Parallel Lines. With reference to your attempt I have nothing, or not much, to observe except that it is incomplete. Your presentation of the proof that the sum of the three angles of a plane triangle cannot be greater than 180° leaves much to be desired in respect of geometrical rigour. This in itself could be remedied, and beyond all doubt the impossibility can be proved most rigorously. Things stand otherwise in the second part, that the sum of the angles cannot be less than 180° ; this is the crucial

3

point, the reef on which all the wrecks take place. I imagine
that you have not been long occupied with this subject. My
own interest in it has extended over 30 years, and I do not
think that anyone can have occupied himself more with this
second part than I, although I have never published anything
on it. The assumption that the sum of the three angles of
a triangle is less than 180° leads to a peculiar Geometry entirely
different from ours,—a geometry completely self-consistent,
which I have developed for myself perfectly satisfactorily, so
that I can solve any problem in it with the assumption that a
constant is determinate, this constant not being capable of
a priori specification. The greater this constant is assumed to
be, the more nearly is Euclidean Geometry approached; and an
infinite value of the constant makes the two systems coincide.
The theorems of this geometry seem somewhat paradoxical, and
to the lay mind absurd; but continued steady reflexion shows
them to contain nothing at all impossible. Thus, for instance,
the three angles of a triangle can be as small as we please, if
only the sides are taken sufficiently great; and yet the area of
a triangle can never exceed a definite limit, however great the
sides are taken to be, and indeed can never reach it. All my
efforts to discover a contradiction, an inconsistency, in this non-
Euclidean Geometry have been unsuccessful; and the one thing
in it contrary to our conceptions is that, were the system true,
there must exist in space a linear magnitude, determined for
itself albeit unknown to us. But methinks, despite the say-
nothing word-wisdom of the metaphysicians, we know far too
little, too nearly nothing, about the true nature of space, for
us to confuse what has an unnatural appearance with what is
absolutely impossible. If the non-Euclidean Geometry were
true, and that constant at all comparable with such magnitudes
as lie within reach of our measurements on the earth or in
the heavens, it could be determined *a posteriori*. Hence I have
sometimes expressed in jest the wish that the Euclidean
Geometry were not true, since then we should possess an
absolute standard of measurement *a priori*. I am not afraid
that a man who has shown himself to possess a thoughtful
mathematical mind will misunderstand the foregoing; but in any

case, please regard this as a private communication, of which public use, or use leading to publicity, is not to be made in any way. If at some future time I acquire more leisure than in my present circumstances, I shall perhaps publish my investigations.

Göttingen, November 8th, 1824."

These investigations continued in the condition of scattered epistolary hints and suggestions until the decease of the foremost mathematician of his day. The solution of any problem, referred to by Gauss as possible for him, is also, at least in principle, possible by the use of the analytical formulae obtained in the First Additional Note at the end of this volume (page 59).

CARNOT

Géométrie de Position, Paris, 1803.

Carnot advocated the Principle of Similitude as an alternative to the Parallel-Postulate, a view-point secured with greater elaboration by Wallis (above, page 18). He wrote (§ 435):

"The Theory of Parallels rests on a primitive idea which seems to me almost of the same degree of clearness as that of perfect equality or of superposition. This is the idea of Similitude. It seems to me that we may regard as a principle of the first rank that what exists on a large scale, as a ball, a house, or a picture, can be reduced in size, and *vice versâ*; and that consequently, for any figure we please to consider, it is possible to imagine others of all sizes similar to it; that is to say, such that all their dimensions continue to be in the same proportions. This idea once admitted, it is easy to establish the Theory of Parallels without resorting to the idea of infinity."

W. BOLYAI

Theoria Parallelarum, Maros-Vasarheli, 1804;
Kurzer Grundriss, 1851.

In the earlier of these tracts, reprinted in the 49th volume of *Mathematische Annalen* (pages 168–204), the elder Bolyai began by supposing an inverted T-square to slide along a straight line. What is the curve described by the upper end of it?

The discussion of this equidistant line in a rather awkward manner led the Hungarian Geometer to a conviction of the validity of Euclidean Geometry.

In the second tract was introduced an ingenious substitute for the Parallel-Postulate:

Let it be conceded that "if three points are not in a straight line, then they lie on a sphere": and therefore on a circle.

To prove from this the principle of the Parallel-Postulate, let A, B, A' be the three points. Let M, M' be the middle points of AB, BA'; and MN, $M'N'$ drawn perpendicular to them. Then the sum of the angles $M'MN$, $MM'N'$ is less than two right angles by the sum of the angles BMM', $BM'M$. Now MN and $M'N'$ must meet, in the centre of the circle (or sphere), unless ABA' is straight. That is, however close the sum of the angles $M'MN$, $MM'N'$ is to two right angles, MN and $M'N'$ intersect. Q.E.D.

The elder Bolyai did not entertain the possibility of MN, $M'N'$ continuing to intersect when ABA' is one straight line; nor did his brilliant son work out the elliptic hypothesis. Like Lobachewski, the younger Bolyai only elaborated a hyperbolic geometry. They both however discussed the properties of curves (L-lines, horocycles) neither rectilinear nor circular, whereof the normals are parallel. Only in Euclidean Geometry is the straight line the limit of a circle of indefinitely increased radius.

THIBAUT

Grundriss der reinen Mathematik, Göttingen, 1809.

Any treatment of parallelism based upon the idea of direction assumes that translation and rotation are independent operations, and this is only so in Euclidean Geometry. The following is the easiest and most plausible way of establishing the parabolic hypothesis. From Euc. I. 32 can be deduced very readily the Euclidean theory of parallelism. Thibaut argued for this theorem as follows:

" Let ABC be any triangle whose sides are traversed in order from A along AB, BC, CA. While going from A to B we always gaze in the direction ABb (AB being produced to b), but do not turn round. On arriving at B we turn from the direction Bb by a rotation through the angle bBC, until we gaze in the direction BCc. Then we proceed in the direction BCc as far as C, where again we turn from Cc to CAa through the angle cCA; and at last arriving at A, we turn from the direction Aa to the first direction AB through the external angle aAB. This done, we have made a complete revolution,— just as if, standing at some point, we had turned completely round; and the measure of this rotation is 2π. Hence the external angles of the triangle add up to 2π, and the internal angles $A + B + C = \pi$. Q.E.D."

TAURINUS

Theorie der Parallel-linien, 1825.

Taurinus expressed eight objections to the wider range of Geometry then being manifested (Engel and Stäckel, pages 208–9).

" 1. It contradicts all intuition. It is true that such a system would in small figures present the same appearance as the Euclidean; but if the conception of space is to be regarded as the pure form of what is indicated by the senses, then the Euclidean system is incontestably the true one, and it cannot be assumed that a limited experience could give rise to actual illusion."

None the less, however, measurement of angles, if sufficiently exact, might deal a fatal blow to Euclid's *a priori* system, by subverting Euc. I. 32.

" 2.   The Euclidean system is the limit of the first system, wherein the angles of a triangle are more than two right angles. With this procedure to the limit, the paradox in connexion with the axiom of the straight line ceases."

In fact Taurinus did not overcome the difficulty universally experienced in respect of the elliptic hypothesis.   Further on he wrote (Engel and Stäckel, page 257):

" In this theorem (51) it is proved that with the assumption that the angle-sum of a quadrilateral can be greater than four right angles (or, what comes to the same thing, if the angle-sum of a triangle can be greater than two right angles), then all the lines, perpendicular to another line, intersect in two points at equal distance on either side.   Hence arises the evident contradiction of the axiom of the straight line, and so such a geometrical system cannot be rectilinear."

To continue :

" 3.   Were the third system the true one, there would be no Euclidean Geometry, whereas however the possibility of the latter cannot be denied."

Certainly the possibility of the Euclidean system cannot be denied, but its actuality may be doubted.   It is so infinitely special an hypothesis.   By way of analogy, does a single comet in the universe possess a strictly parabolic orbit ?

" 4.   In the assumption of such a system as rectilinear, there is no continuous transition ; the angles of a triangle could only make more or less than two right angles."

The Euclidean system, nevertheless, is the connecting link desired between the elliptic and hyperbolic geometries.   It is the limit of each ; whether it separates them or unites them is only a matter of words.

" 5.   These systems would have quite paradoxical conse-quences, contradicting all our conceptions ; we should have to assign to space properties it cannot have."

This appeal to commonsense is of value in practical work, where close approximation suffices.

" 6. All complete similarity of surfaces and bodies would be wanting; and still this idea seems to have its roots in intuition, and to be a true postulate."

The view of some of the world's greatest thinkers,—and they have Wallis for spokesman.

" 7. The Euclidean system is in any case the most complete, and its truth therefore possesses the greatest plausibility."

But all three hypotheses together supply a more complete Theory of Space than any single one of them, and their common basis is the assumption that space is homogeneous. More complete still will be the Geometry of the future, contemplating a heterogeneous space (compare Clifford's speculation; below, page 49).

" 8. The internal consistency of the third system is no reason for regarding it as a rectilinear system; however, there is in it, so far as we know, no contradiction of the axiom of the straight line as in the first."

These objections are mainly of an *a priori* character. On the other hand, our knowledge of space as an objectivity is small. Increased precision of astronomical instruments might display antipodal images of a few bright stars, and this would then tell in favour of an elliptic hypothesis. The space-constant is large, very large; but no experiment can ever prove it infinite, as Euclideans assume it.

J. BOLYAI

*Appendix scientiam spatii exhibens...*Maros-Vasarheli, 1832.

English, German and French translations have been made of this brilliant tractate by Halsted, Frischauf and Hoüel, the first under the title *Science Absolute of Space* (Austin, Texas, 1896). Bolyai gave independently therein a clear, brief, and sound introduction to the study of the hyperbolic hypothesis. Only a summary description is necessary, as the student will prefer to peruse its 43 paragraphs for himself. Starting from the strict definition of a parallel as the limiting position of a secant, Bolyai proceeded to solid geometry, and deduced the existence of *L*-lines and *F*-surfaces (called by Lobachewski *horocycles* and *horospheres*), which are the limiting forms of circles and spheres of infinite radius in hyperbolic space. He found Euclidean geometry to obtain for horocycles drawn on horospheres; but for rectilinear triangles drawn on a plane, he proved that the area was proportional to the supplement of the angle-sum (§ 43). The work merits careful study, and comparison with the corresponding work of Lobachewski.

LEGENDRE

Réflexions sur...la Théorie des Parallèles, Paris, 1833.

Although Dr Heath has given a very full account of this contribution of Legendre's to the *Mémoires de l'Institut de France* (Vol. 12, pages 367–390), the following notes on the work of this most popular Geometer afford opportunities for independent criticisms. We find Legendre writing:

"After some researches undertaken with the aim of proving directly that the sum of the angles of a triangle is equal to two right angles, I have succeeded first in proving that this sum cannot be greater than two right angles. Here is the proof as it appeared for the first time in the 3rd edition of my Geometry published in 1800."

The proof proceeded thus: Let $P_1Q_1Q_2$, $P_2Q_2Q_3$, $P_3Q_3Q_4$ ... be a series of identically equal triangles with their bases Q_1Q_2, Q_2Q_3, Q_3Q_4 ... collinear and contiguous, and their vertices P_1, P_2, P_3 ... on the same side of their bases. If the angle-sum of a triangle exceeds a straight angle, the angle $Q_1P_1Q_2$ exceeds the angle $P_1Q_2P_2$. Therefore $P_1P_2 < Q_1Q_2$ (Euc. I. 18).

Let this difference be x. Then if n is a number such that nx is greater than the sum of the two sides of any one of the congruent triangles, supposed now to be n in number,

$$Q_1Q_{n+1} > Q_1P_1 + P_1P_2 + P_2P_3 + \ldots + P_{n-1}P_n + P_nQ_{n+1},$$

i.e. the straight line is not the shortest distance between the two points Q_1 and Q_{n+1}.

The solution of this enigma is that the elliptic hypothesis was actually assumed; and for this hypothesis, the straight line is re-entrant, and Q_{n+1} may fall, for instance, between Q_1 and Q_2.

Legendre then proceeded further:

"The first proposition being established, it remained to prove that the sum of the angles cannot be less than two right angles; but we must confess that this second proposition, though the principle of its proof was well-known (see Note II, page 298, of the 12th Edition of the *Elements of Geometry*), has presented difficulties which we have not been able entirely to clear away. This it is which caused us, in the 9th Edition, to return to Euclid's procedure; and later, in the 12th, to adopt another method of proof to be spoken of hereafter....It is doubtless due to the imperfection of popular language, and the difficulty of giving a good definition of the straight line, that Geometers have hitherto achieved little success, when they endeavoured to deduce this Theorem (Euc. I. 32) from ideas purely based on the equality of triangles contained in the First Book of the Elements."

The notion that the definition of the straight line was in some way the *nodus* of the Theory of Parallelism had evidently occurred to Taurinus and others, and was expressed as a conviction by Dodgson in his *New Theory of Parallels* (1895). But contrast Lobachewski's judgment (below, page 43).

Legendre then gave a proof of Euc. I. 32 "as it appeared for the first time in the 1st Edition of my *Geometry*, published in 1794, and as reproduced in the Editions following." This was based on the following reasoning:

By superposition it appears that two triangles are congruent if their bases and both base-angles are equal, each to each. That is, a, B, C determine the triangle ABC uniquely. Hence $A = f(B, C, a)$. Therefore $a = F(A, B, C)$, say. But A, B, C are pure numbers, if the right angle is taken for unit-angle. Hence a is obtained as a pure number. This is in fact the paradox remarked upon by Gauss in his letter to Taurinus (above, page 34). Only in the exceptional case when a does not enter at all into the equation $A = f(B, C, a)$, e.g. when $A = \pi - B - C$, is there no unit of length associated with any unit of angle.

Legendre next gave an ingenious and elaborate proof that if the angle-sum of one triangle in the plane is π, the angle-sum of every triangle is π. He observed further that if the angle-sum of a triangle were greater (less) than π, then equidistants would be convex (concave) to their bases; but failed to make cogent use of this apparent paradox, as it then was.

His last attempt to dispose of the elliptic hypothesis by manipulation of the figure of Euc. I. 16 was effected with much greater elegance by Lobachewski (below, page 44). Legendre's construction and argument are given by Dr Heath in the first volume of his *Elements* (page 215).

LOBACHEWSKI

Geometrische Untersuchungen zur Theorie der Parallel-linien,
Berlin, 1840.

As Dr Whitehead has said in one of his tracts:
" Metrical Geometry of the hyperbolic type was first discovered by Lobachewski in 1826, and independently by J. Bolyai in 1832. This discovery is the origin of the modern period of thought in respect of the foundations of Geometry " (*Axioms of Descriptive Geometry*, page 71).
The *Geometrische Untersuchungen* has been done into English by Halsted (Austin, Texas, 1891).

Characterising Legendre's efforts as fruitless, the Russian Geometer went on to say:
" My first essay on the foundations of Geometry was published in the Kasan *Messenger* for the year 1829....I will here give the substance of my investigations, remarking that, contrary to the

opinion of Legendre, all other imperfections, for instance, the definition of a straight line, are foreign to the argument, and without real influence upon the Theory of Parallels."

Then followed a number of simple theorems, independent of any particular theory of parallelism, although the third presents the appearance of contradicting the elliptic hypothesis, thus:

"A straight line sufficiently prolonged on both sides proceeds beyond every limit (über jede Grenze), and so separates a limited plane into two parts."

The ninth of Lobachewski's preliminaries, however, did distinctly assume a theorem not universally valid for the elliptic hypothesis:

" In the rectilinear triangle, a greater angle lies opposite the greater side."

The sixteenth step inaugurated the Hyperbolic Hypothesis:

" 16. All straight lines issuing from a point in a plane can be divided, with reference to a given straight line in this plane, into two classes, namely, *secant* and *asecant*. The limiting straight line between one class and the other is called *parallel* to the given straight line."

Thus if MH is a parallel to NB on one side of the perpendicular MN let fall from M upon NB, then the angle HMN was called the *angle of parallelism*. Let the length of MN be p, and denote by ϖ the corresponding angle of parallelism HMN, then Lobachewski established rigorously the very curious result:

The complement of ϖ is the Gudermannian of p/K, where K is constant over the plane.

Thus the angle of parallelism was determined in all cases; and Lobachewski's result was identical with that obtained above on page xviii

$$\sin \varpi = \operatorname{sech} p/K. \quad -$$

Lobachewski's proof was intricate, however, and involved the horocycles and horospheres mentioned already (page 40).

Very elegant is Lobachewski's application of the construction of Euc. I. 16 (itself a pattern of elegance) to prove that the angle-sum of a triangle cannot exceed two right angles. Let ABC be the triangle, and let its angle-sum be $\pi + \epsilon$. Take the least side BC, and bisect it in D. Join AD, and produce to E, so that DE is equal in length to AD. Then the triangles CDE, BDA are superposable. Hence the angle-sum of the triangle ACE is $\pi + \epsilon$. Now by bisecting the side opposite the least angle, and continuing Euclid's construction indefinitely for each new triangle obtained, two of the angles can at length be reduced to magnitudes each less than $\dfrac{\epsilon}{2}$; and thus, since the angle-sum of each triangle is $\pi + \epsilon$, the third angle must finally exceed π.

There is nevertheless no serious difficulty, provided space is of finite size, as Riemann suggested later.

MEIKLE

Theory of Parallel Lines, Edinburgh, 1844.

The work of Henry Meikle, published in the *Edinburgh New Philosophical Journal* (Vol. 36, pages 310–318), merits special attention for its sound character, comparative obscurity, and subsequent fertility in the hands of Kelland (*Transactions R. S. E.*, Vol. 23, pages 433–450) and Chrystal (*Non-Euclidean Geometry*, Edinburgh, 1880).

The memoir commenced:

"During the long succession of ages which have elapsed since the origin of Geometry, many attempts have been made and treatises written, though with little success, to demonstrate the important Theorem which Euclid, having failed to prove, has styled his 12th Axiom, and which is nearly equivalent to assuming that the three angles of every triangle amount to two right angles."

Except that the elliptic hypothesis is not excluded by the Parallel-Postulate, one might say " exactly equivalent."

The excellence of Meikle's work, and its supreme originality, are attached to an ingenious and effective Construction, of which some use was made without acknowledgment in the Appendix to our *Euclid, Book I. with a Commentary.* This Construction affords a demonstration of the Theorem that triangles of equal areas have equal angle-sums. Thus:

Let ABC be any triangle, and D, E the middle points of the sides AC, AB. Draw AL, BM, CN perpendicular to DE. Then the triangles BME, ALE are congruent; and so are the triangles ALD, CND. Hence the quadrilateral $BCMN$ has both its area and its angle-sum equal to those of the triangle ABC.

Thus, reversing the construction, a triangle of equal area and angle-sum can be constructed having a side BA' of any desired length not less than twice BM; and then on BA' as base can be constructed an isosceles triangle of equal area and angle-sum. In this way, two triangles of equal areas can be reduced to isosceles triangles of the same areas and angle-sums; and on the same base. But isosceles triangles of equal areas on the same base must coincide entirely. Hence the two original triangles with areas equal have also their angle-sums equal. Q.E.D.

By the aid of this magnificent piece of reasoning, Meikle proved that the area of a triangle is proportional to what has been called its divergence; but he rejected the hyperbolic hypothesis on the ground that it involved triangles of finite area with zero angles,—the paradox which aroused Gauss' interest (above, page 33).

BOUNIAKOWSKI

Mémoires de l'Académie...de St Pétersbourg, 1850.

This writer criticised the work of Legendre and Bertrand, and endeavoured to improve upon it. He presented a simple proof of the Parallel-Postulate in the following form:

Let *MNP* be a transversal crossing *MA*, *NB*; and making the angles *AMN*, *BNM* together less than two right angles. Then the angle *BNP* is greater than the angle *AMP*; and therefore the infinite sector *BNP* is of greater area than the infinite sector *AMP*. Now if *MA* did not meet *NB*, the infinite sector *BNP* would be contained wholly within the infinite sector *AMP*, and so would be of less area. Therefore *MA* cannot but meet *NB*.

If however we try to draw a figure introducing the infinitely distant regions in any reasonable way, the proof collapses entirely. Far more powerful and forcible is Bertrand's demonstration given above (page 28).

RIEMANN

Habilitationsrede, 1854.

Riemann's brief but brilliant and epoch-making Essay was translated by Clifford (*Collected Papers,* page 56). The possible combination of finite size and unbounded extent, as properties of space, was indicated in the words:

"In the extension of space-construction to the infinitely great, we must distinguish between *unboundedness* and *infinite extent*; the former belongs to the descriptive category, the latter to the metrical. That space is an unbounded threefold manifoldness is an assumption that is developed by every conception of the outer world....The unboundedness of space possesses...a greater empirical certainty than any external experience. But its infinite extent by no means follows from this; on the contrary, if we assume bodies independent of position, and therefore ascribe to space constant curvature, it must necessarily be finite, provided this curvature has ever so small a value."

The expression *curvature of space* is an unfortunate metaphor, derived from the analogy between the elliptic geometry of the plane and the parabolic geometry of surfaces of uniform curvature. The plane is not curved for the elliptic, nor for the hyperbolic hypothesis. Considerable misconception has arisen in this way. The study of Beltrami's analogies rectifies such an error.

Riemann further noted the conceivable heterogeneity of space. The space-constant may be different in different places. It may also vary with the time.

CAYLEY

Sixth Memoir upon Quantics, London, 1859.

Cayley developed an analytical theory of Metric which could be coordinated to the three hypotheses which constitute the geometry of a homogeneous space. The hypotheses presented themselves as the three cases when the straight line has no, one, or two real points at infinite distance from all other points on itself. These three cases are allied to the hypotheses of no, one, or two parallels from a given point to the straight line.

VON HELMHOLTZ

The Essential Principles of Geometry, 1866, 1868.

Von Helmholtz endeavoured to give new and precise expression to the Axioms or Postulates upon which a science of spatial relationships could be constructed, e.g. perfectly free moveability of rigid bodies. The whole of the ground has been gone over with great thoroughness by succeeding Geometers, notably Lie. The final results of these labours have been summarised by Dr Whitehead in his *Tracts.*

BELTRAMI

Attempt to interpret non-Euclidean Geometry, 1868.

Beltrami's *Saggio*, of which a French translation was made by Hoüel (*Annales de l'École Normale Supérieure*, Vol. 6, pages 251–288), is of supreme importance in the development of the Science of Space. The Italian Geometer proved conclusively the right of the elliptic and hyperbolic hypotheses to rank equally with the Euclidean system as theories of a homogeneous space ; and, empirically, they are clearly superior. Beltrami showed this by pointing out that all the elliptic (and hyperbolic) geometry of the plane was characterised by the same metrical relationships as hold good in the parabolic geometry of surfaces of uniform positive (and negative) curvature. Any flaw in the former would necessarily be accompanied by a flaw in the latter. If there is no flaw in the Euclidean geometry of geodesics on a surface of uniform curvature, then there can be no flaw in the metabolic geometry of straight lines on a plane surface, for the metrical relationships are identical. This conclusive argument can scarcely be refuted ; Poincaré does not meet it in his *La Science et l'Hypothèse*. It was therefore Beltrami's labours which first established Non-Euclidean Geometry on the firm foundation whereon it rests to-day, despite every kind of prejudice and misconception which it has encountered hitherto.

CLIFFORD

The Space-Theory of Matter, 1870.

Somewhat beyond theories of parallelism, but suggestive like everything else of his, the fragment of Clifford's here reproduced shows the freedom of the Geometer released from the fetters of traditionalism. It is chosen from a paper embodied in his *Collected Works* (page 22):

"I wish here to indicate a manner in which these specula-
tions (of Riemann's) may be applied to the investigation of
physical phenomena. I hold in fact:

"(1) That small portions of space are of a nature analogous
to little hills on a surface which is on the average flat; namely,
that the ordinary laws of geometry are not valid in them.

"(2) That this property of being curved or distorted is
continually passed on from one portion of space to another after
the manner of a wave.

"(3) That this variation of the curvature of space is what
really happens in that phenomenon which we call the motion
of matter whether ponderable or ethereal.

"(4) That in the physical world nothing else takes place
but this variation, subject, possibly, to the law of continuity.

"I am endeavouring in a general way to explain the laws of
double refraction on this hypothesis, but have not yet arrived at
any results sufficiently decisive to be communicated."

The boldness of this speculation is surely unexcelled in the
history of thought. Up to the present, however, it presents the
appearance of an Icarian flight.

KLEIN

Ueber die sogenannte nicht-Euklidische Geometrie, 1871.

To Dr Felix Klein, Professor at Göttingen, are owed two
monographs (*Mathematische Annalen,* Vol. 4, pages 573–625;
Vol. 6, pages 112–145), which have been followed up by two
volumes of lectures on non-Euclidean Geometry. The names of
Cayley, Clifford and Klein will always be associated with a
certain view-point, which may be styled the analytical theory
of metrical relations.

In the first of his classical Memoirs Dr Klein introduced
that terminology which has won its way to general acceptance:

"The three Geometries have been called *hyperbolic*, *elliptic*, and *parabolic*, respectively, according as the two infinitely distant points of the straight line are real, imaginary, and coincident" (see page 47 above).

The second paragraph opens thus:
"All spatial metric rests upon two fundamental problems, as we know: the determination of the distance of two points and of the inclination of two straight lines."

The fundamental laws of linear and angular measurement are, in fact: $\overline{xy} + \overline{yz} = \overline{xz}$, with the proviso that $\overline{xx} = 0$; so that $\overline{xy} + \overline{yx} = \overline{xx} = 0$, and therefore $\overline{xy} = -\overline{yx}$. These first principles of metric have been discussed in a simple but ingenious way by Sir Robert Stawell Ball in the last chapter of his *Theory of Screws* (Cambridge, 1900).

Klein followed Riemann and Cayley in the use of coordinates to define position, and deduced formulae for lengths and angles from the first principles suggested above. The results, that length and angle are proportional to the logarithms of certain anharmonic ratios estimated with reference to an Absolute formed of infinitely distant elements, cannot be assessed by Euclidean standards, but belong to a higher sphere of research than is here explored. This remark applies also to Klein's second Memoir, and indeed to most of the best modern work in Non-Euclidean Geometry.

NEWCOMB

Elementary Theorems relating to the Geometry of a Space of three Dimensions and of uniform positive Curvature in the fourth Dimension, 1877.

The American Astronomer first assumed the homogeneity of space (*Crelle's Journal*, Vol. 83, pages 293–299). Then:
"2. I assume that this space is affected with such curvature that a right line shall always return into itself at the end

of a finite and real distance $2D$, without losing, in any part of its course, that symmetry with respect to space on all sides of it which constitutes the fundamental property of our conception of it."

This definition of rectilinearity and the assumption of finitude are faultless; but no more needs to be assumed. Newcomb might now have proved that

$$\text{area/divergence} = 4D^2/\pi^2;$$

and the theorem below might have been furnished with a demonstration. Instead of this, however:

"3. I assume that if two right lines emanate from the same point, making the indefinitely small angle α with each other, their distance apart at the distance r from the point of intersection will be given by the equation

$$s = \frac{2\alpha D}{\pi} \sin \frac{r\pi}{2D}."$$

But, as was shown by Dr Chrystal, since area is by (2) necessarily proportional to divergence,

$$s\, dr = d\left(-\frac{4D^2}{\pi^2} \tan^{-1} \frac{ds}{dr}\right),$$

i.e.
$$\frac{d^2s}{dr^2} + \frac{\pi^2 s}{4D^2} = 0.$$

Hence
$$s = A \sin \frac{\pi r}{2D} + B \cos \frac{\pi r}{2D};$$

and when $r \longrightarrow 0$, $s \longrightarrow 0$, and $\dfrac{ds}{dr} \longrightarrow \alpha$: so that

$$B = 0, \quad A = \frac{2D\alpha}{\pi}.$$

Therefore
$$s = \frac{2D\alpha}{\pi} \sin \frac{\pi r}{2D}.$$

DODGSON

A New Theory of Parallels, London, 1895.

The amiable author of *Alice in Wonderland* contributed to the Theory of Parallelism a pretty substitute for the Fifth Postulate, as follows:

" In every circle, the inscribed equilateral tetragon is greater than any one of the segments which lie outside it."

Dodgson's Axiom was aimed at the exclusion of the hyperbolic hypothesis, in which the assertion is not universally correct.

For consider, on the hyperbolic plane, a circle of very great radius nK, where n is a large number, and two perpendicular diameters AOA', BOB'.

The area of the circle is

$$2\pi \int_0^{nK} K \sinh \frac{x}{K}\, dx = 2\pi K^2 (\cosh n - 1),$$

which approaches the limit $\pi K^2 e^n$, as n increases indefinitely.

On the other hand, the area of the quadrilateral formed by the points A, A', B, B' is

$$4K^2 \left\{ \frac{\pi}{2} - 2 \tan^{-1} (\operatorname{sech} n) \right\},$$

because $\cos ABO = \cosh \dfrac{AO}{K} \sin OAB$ (above, page xviii). And as n increases, this approaches the limit

$$2\pi K^2 - 8K^2 \tan^{-1} (2e^{-n}), \quad i.e.\ 2\pi K^2.$$

Whence it appears that the area of a segment is ultimately infinitely greater than the area of the tetragon.

FIRST ADDITIONAL NOTE

ANALYTICAL GEOMETRY FOR THE METABOLIC HYPOTHESES

FROM very simple synthetic results, the most comprehensive analytical formulae for Metabolic Geometry can be secured. These formulae of general application will be proved for the elliptic hypothesis, and the corresponding forms for the hyperbolic hypothesis will be interpolated as occasion arises.

The principal assumptions are (i) that the area of a triangle is k^2 (or K^2) times its divergence, and (ii) that the straight line is in general a line of minimum length between any two of its points. The groundwork of our Introduction, along with an argument similar to that of Euc. I. 16–20, justifies these assumptions, to which may be added the observation that Euclidean geometry holds good within any infinitesimal area of a homogeneous plane.

Adhering then, for convenience, to the Elliptic Hypothesis, let r be the radius vector, θ the vectorial angle, and ϕ the inclination of the tangent to the radius vector for any point of a curve. Let O be the pole, and P, P' the points of contact of two consecutive tangents to the curve, inclined at an infinitesimal angle $d\psi$. Let $R\,d\theta$ be the area of the triangle OPP', where R is a function of r at present unknown. Then by (i), to the first order of infinitesimals,

$$R\,d\theta = k^2\,(d\theta + \pi - \phi + \phi + d\phi + \pi - d\psi - 2\pi)$$
$$= k^2\,(d\theta + d\phi - d\psi).$$

Let t be a parameter for the point P of the curve, then this result becomes

$$\dot{\psi} = \left(1 - \frac{R}{k^2}\right) \dot{\theta} + \dot{\phi}.$$

In particular, for the points of a straight line $\dot{\psi} = 0$, and so

$$\left(1 - \frac{R}{k^2}\right) \dot{\theta} + \dot{\phi} = 0.$$

Again by (ii) we have for the straight line

$$\delta \int \dot{s} \, dt = 0,$$

where s is the length of the arc of the curve measured from one of its points. And the infinitesimal length of the perpendicular from P upon OP' is $R'd\theta$, where the dash denotes differentiation for r,—because the product of dr and $R'd\theta$ gives the correct value $dR\,d\theta$ for the element of area in polar coordinates. Thus, for a straight line,

$$\delta \int \sqrt{\dot{r}^2 + R'^2 \dot{\theta}^2} \, . \, dt = 0.$$

Hence, by the Calculus,

$$\frac{d}{dt} \frac{\dot{r}}{\dot{s}} = \frac{R'R''\dot{\theta}^2}{\dot{s}},$$

and

$$\frac{d}{dt} \frac{R'^2 \dot{\theta}}{\dot{s}} = 0,$$

where dots denote differentiation for the parameter t.

But

$$\cos \phi = \frac{\dot{r}}{\dot{s}}, \quad \sin \phi = \frac{R'\dot{\theta}}{\dot{s}},$$

so that we have

$$\frac{d}{dt} (\cos \phi) = R''\dot{\theta} \sin \phi, \quad \frac{d}{dt} (R' \sin \phi) = 0.$$

Thus $\dot{\phi} = -R''\dot{\theta}$, $R' \sin \phi = P'$, where P' is the value assumed by the function R' when $r = p$, p being the perpendicular from O on the straight line. These two results are not independent, of course.

But, for a straight line, $k^2\dot\phi + (k^2 - R)\,\dot\theta = 0$.

Therefore $k^2 R'' + R - k^2 = 0$; and by differentiation for r,

$$k^2 R''' + R' = 0.$$

Integrating, $R' = L\cos\dfrac{r}{k} + M\sin\dfrac{r}{k}$, where L and M are independent of r.

Remembering that for $r = 0$, $R' = 0$; and that for r small, $R' = r$, we see that $R' = k\sin\dfrac{r}{k}$.

Hence for the straight line, as considered,

$$k\sin\frac{r}{k}\sin\phi = k\sin\frac{p}{k};$$

that is, in a right-angled triangle of hypothenuse r, wherein p is the length of the side opposite the angle ϕ,

$$\sin\frac{r}{k}\sin\phi = \sin\frac{p}{k}.$$

[For the Hyperbolic Hypothesis, $\sinh\dfrac{r}{K}\sin\phi = \sinh\dfrac{p}{K}$.

Also we find now for any curve

$$\left.\begin{aligned}
ds^2 &= dr^2 + k^2\sin^2\frac{r}{k}\cdot d\theta^2, \\
\tan\phi &= k\sin\frac{r}{k}\cdot\frac{d\theta}{dr}, \\
\dot\psi &= \cos\frac{r}{k}\cdot\dot\theta + \dot\phi.
\end{aligned}\right\}$$

[For the Hyperbolic Hypothesis,

$$\left.\begin{aligned}
ds^2 &= dr^2 + K^2\sinh^2\frac{r}{K}\cdot d\theta^2, \\
\tan\phi &= K\sinh\frac{r}{K}\cdot\frac{d\theta}{dr}, \\
\dot\psi &= \cosh\frac{r}{K}\cdot\dot\theta + \dot\phi.
\end{aligned}\right\}$$

We prove next that $\tan \dfrac{p}{k} = \tan \dfrac{r}{k} \cos \theta$.

In fact, $\dfrac{d\theta}{dr} = \dfrac{1}{k} \operatorname{cosec} \dfrac{r}{k} \tan \phi$; and $\sin \phi = \sin \dfrac{p}{k} \operatorname{cosec} \dfrac{r}{k}$;

so that

$$k \frac{d\theta}{dr} = \operatorname{cosec} \frac{r}{k} \frac{\sin \dfrac{p}{k}}{\sqrt{\sin^2 \dfrac{r}{k} - \sin^2 \dfrac{p}{k}}}$$

$$= \operatorname{cosec}^2 \frac{r}{k} \bigg/ \sqrt{\operatorname{cosec}^2 \frac{p}{k} - \operatorname{cosec}^2 \frac{r}{k}}$$

$$= \operatorname{cosec}^2 \frac{r}{k} \bigg/ \sqrt{\cot^2 \frac{p}{k} - \cot^2 \frac{r}{k}};$$

whence $\qquad \theta - \alpha = \cos^{-1}\left(\cot \dfrac{r}{k} \bigg/ \cot \dfrac{p}{k} \right);$

and so $\qquad \tan \dfrac{p}{k} = \tan \dfrac{r}{k} \cos (\theta - \alpha).$

[For the Hyperbolic Hypothesis, $\tanh \dfrac{p}{K} = \tanh \dfrac{r}{K} \cos (\theta - \alpha)$.]

Hence if the perpendicular p from O upon any straight line is inclined at angle α to the axis Ox from which the vectorial angle θ is measured,

$$\tan \frac{p}{k} = \tan \frac{r}{k} \cos (\theta - \alpha).$$

We can next find the length $P'P''$ between the points $(r'\theta')$ and $(r''\theta'')$. Using the result just obtained, along with $\dot{s} = k \sin \dfrac{r}{k} \operatorname{cosec} \phi \cdot \dot{\theta}$, we get

$$P'P'' = k \tan \frac{p}{k} \sec \frac{p}{k} \int_{\theta'}^{\theta''} \frac{d\theta}{\cos^2(\theta - \alpha) + \tan^2 \dfrac{p}{k}}.$$

Adopting $\tan \dfrac{p}{k} \tan (\theta - \alpha)$ for variable, and integrating,

$$P'P'' = k \int_{\theta'}^{\theta''} \tan^{-1} \left\{ \sin \frac{p}{k} \tan (\theta - \alpha) \right\}.$$

I.e., $\qquad \tan \dfrac{P'P''}{k} = \dfrac{\sin \dfrac{p}{k}\,(\tan \overline{\theta'' - \alpha} - \tan \overline{\theta' - \alpha})}{1 + \sin^2 \dfrac{p}{k} \tan (\theta' - \alpha) \tan (\theta'' - \alpha)},$

a result presently transformed into

$$\cos \frac{P'P''}{k} = \cos \frac{r'}{k} \cos \frac{r''}{k} + \sin \frac{r'}{k} \sin \frac{r''}{k} \cos (\theta' - \theta''),$$

which manifests the analogy between the elliptic geometry of the plane and the parabolic geometry of the sphere.

[For the Hyperbolic Hypothesis,

$$\cosh \frac{P'P''}{K} = \cosh \frac{r'}{K} \cosh \frac{r''}{K} - \sinh \frac{r'}{K} \sinh \frac{r''}{K} \cos (\theta' - \theta'').$$

Let us now adopt Escherich's Coordinates. Let Ox, Oy be two perpendicular axes ; PM and PN the perpendiculars upon them from any point P ; and write $x = \tan \dfrac{OM}{k}, \ y = \tan \dfrac{ON}{k}.$

[For the Hyperbolic Hypothesis, $x = \tanh \dfrac{OM}{K}, \ y = \tanh \dfrac{ON}{K}.$

We then have at once

$$\cos \frac{PP'}{k} = \frac{1 + xx' + yy'}{\sqrt{1 + x^2 + y^2} \, \sqrt{1 + x'^2 + y'^2}} \quad \ldots\ldots\ldots\ldots(\text{I}).$$

[For the Hyperbolic Hypothesis,

$$\cosh \frac{PP'}{K} = \frac{1 - xx' - yy'}{\sqrt{1 - x^2 - y^2} \, \sqrt{1 - x'^2 - y'^2}}.$$

Choosing consecutive points, $x' = x + dx, \ y' = y + dy,$ we have

$$ds^2 = k^2 \frac{dx^2 + dy^2 + (xdy - ydx)^2}{(1 + x^2 + y^2)^2}.$$

[For the Hyperbolic Hypothesis,

$$ds^2 = K^2 \frac{dx^2 + dy^2 - (xdy - ydx)^2}{(1 - x^2 - y^2)^2}.$$

Also, from $\tan \dfrac{p}{k} = \tan \dfrac{r}{k} \cos(\theta - \alpha)$, obtained above, we now have

$$\tan \frac{r}{k} \cos\theta \cos\alpha + \tan \frac{r}{k} \cos\left(\frac{\pi}{2} - \theta\right) \sin\alpha = \tan\frac{p}{k},$$

showing that the equation of the straight line in these coordinates is $x \cos\alpha + y \sin\alpha = $ constant; or, in general,

$$ax + by + c = 0 \quad \ldots\ldots\ldots\ldots\ldots\ldots\ldots\text{(II)}$$

where a, b, c are any constants.

We may next determine the angle of intersection of the two straight lines $ax + by + c = 0$, $a'x + b'y + c' = 0$.

Let P be their point of intersection, with coordinates x, y; and Q, Q' consecutive points of the two lines, with coordinates $(x + \epsilon b,\ y - \epsilon a)$ and $(x + \epsilon'b',\ y - \epsilon'a')$, where ϵ and ϵ' are very small.

Then the angle χ required is determinable from the application of the Euclidean formula to the infinitesimal triangle QPQ',

$$QQ'^2 = PQ^2 + PQ'^2 - 2PQ \cdot PQ' \cdot \cos QPQ'.$$

Hence, omitting a common denominator,

$$(\epsilon b - \epsilon'b')^2 + (\epsilon a - \epsilon'a')^2 + (x \cdot \overline{\epsilon a - \epsilon'a'} + y \cdot \overline{\epsilon b - \epsilon'b'})^2$$
$$= (\epsilon b)^2 + (\epsilon a)^2 + (x \cdot \epsilon a + y \cdot \epsilon b)^2 + (\epsilon'b')^2 + (\epsilon'a')^2$$
$$+ (x \cdot \epsilon'a' + y \cdot \epsilon'b')^2 - 2\cos\chi$$
$$\times \sqrt{\epsilon^2 b^2 + \epsilon^2 a^2 + (\epsilon ax + \epsilon by)^2} \cdot \sqrt{\epsilon'^2 b'^2 + \epsilon'^2 a'^2 + (\epsilon'a'x + \epsilon'b'y)^2}.$$

But $ax + by = -c$, and $a'x + b'y = -c'$; and so

$$\cos\chi = \frac{aa' + bb' + cc'}{\sqrt{a^2 + b^2 + c^2} \cdot \sqrt{a'^2 + b'^2 + c'^2}} \quad \ldots\ldots\ldots\text{(III)}.$$

[For the Hyperbolic Hypothesis,

$$\cos\chi = \frac{aa' + bb' - cc'}{\sqrt{a^2 + b^2 - c^2} \cdot \sqrt{a'^2 + b'^2 - c'^2}}.$$

In particular, then, the straight lines are perpendicular, if

$$aa' + bb' + cc' = 0.$$

[For the Hyperbolic Hypothesis,

$$aa' + bb' - cc' = 0.$$

Calling u, v the coordinates of a straight line $ux + vy - 1 = 0$, the angle between the consecutive lines (u, v) $(u + du, v + dv)$ is given by

$$d\chi^2 = \frac{du^2 + dv^2 + (udv - vdu)^2}{(1 + u^2 + v^2)^2}.$$

[For the Hyperbolic Hypothesis,

$$d\chi^2 = \frac{du^2 + dv^2 - (udv - vdu)^2}{(1 - u^2 - v^2)^2}.$$

We now only need further (and only for convenience' sake) to determine the length of the perpendicular p' from $(x'y')$ upon $ax + by + c = 0$. This is derivable from results I, II and III; suggesting that these contain the entire metric of the elliptic plane in analytical form. The coordinates of the foot of the perpendicular are found by II and III to be

$$\left(\frac{Dx' - P'a}{D - P'c}, \ \frac{Dy' - P'b}{D - P'c} \right),$$

where $D \equiv a^2 + b^2 + c^2$, $P' \equiv ax' + by' + c$.

Thus $\cos \dfrac{p'}{k} = \sqrt{\dfrac{D(1 + x'^2 + y'^2) - P'^2}{(1 + x'^2 + y'^2)D}}$,

whence $\sin \dfrac{p'}{k} = \dfrac{ax' + by' + c}{\sqrt{a^2 + b^2 + c^2}\sqrt{1 + x'^2 + y'^2}}$ ....(IV).

[For the Hyperbolic Hypothesis,

$$\sinh \frac{p'}{K} = \frac{ax' + by' + c}{\sqrt{a^2 + b^2 - c^2}\sqrt{1 - x'^2 - y'^2}}.$$

Any problem in Metabolic Geometry may be attacked by means of results I—IV thus secured.

For instance, the equation of a Circle of centre $(\xi\eta)$ and radius ρ is by I

$$(1 + \xi x + \eta y)^2 = \cos^2 \frac{\rho}{k} \cdot (1 + \xi^2 + \eta^2)(1 + x^2 + y^2).$$

[For the Hyperbolic Hypothesis,

$$(1 - \xi x - \eta y)^2 = \cosh^2 \frac{\rho}{K} \cdot (1 - \xi^2 - \eta^2)(1 - x^2 - y^2).$$

[Letting $\xi = 0$, $\eta = \tanh \frac{\rho}{K}$, and ρ become indefinitely great, the equation of a Horocycle touching Ox at O is obtained:

$$(1 - y)^2 = 1 - x^2 - y^2.$$

The equation to an Equidistant of axis $ax + by + c = 0$ at distance ϖ is by IV

$$(ax + by + c)^2 = \sin^2 \frac{\varpi}{k} \cdot (a^2 + b^2 + c^2)(1 + x^2 + y^2).$$

[For the Hyperbolic Hypothesis,

$$(ax + by + c)^2 = \sinh^2 \frac{\varpi}{K} \cdot (a^2 + b^2 - c^2)(1 - x^2 - y^2).$$

A result of considerable beauty and interest is an expression for the measure of curvature. If $d\epsilon$ is the angle between the normals at the extremities of an infinitesimal arc ds of any curve, and the radius of curvature ρ is defined by $\frac{ds}{d\epsilon} = k \sin \frac{\rho}{k}$, then if t is the parameter of a point on the curve, formulae I and III give

$$\cot \frac{\rho}{k} = (\dot{x}\ddot{y} - \ddot{x}\dot{y}) \left\{ \frac{1 + x^2 + y^2}{\dot{x}^2 + \dot{y}^2 + (x\dot{y} - \dot{x}y)^2} \right\}^{\frac{3}{2}}.$$

[For the Hyperbolic Hypothesis,

$$\coth \frac{\rho}{K} = (\dot{x}\ddot{y} - \ddot{x}\dot{y}) \left\{ \frac{1 - x^2 - y^2}{\dot{x}^2 + \dot{y}^2 - (x\dot{y} - \dot{x}y)^2} \right\}^{\frac{3}{2}}.$$

Applied to the equation of the equidistant to Ox at distance δ, namely:

$$y^2 = (1 + x^2) \tan^2 \frac{\delta}{k},$$

or parametrically,

$$x = \tan t, \quad y = \tan \frac{\delta}{k} \cdot \sec t,$$

the curvature-formula gives

$$\cot \frac{\rho}{k} = \tan \frac{\delta}{k},$$

suggesting that the curve is a circle of radius $\frac{\pi k}{2} - \delta$.

Evidently the results given in this brief Note are sufficient to furnish occupation for innumerable leisure hours, in the extension of the usual results of Analytical Geometry to the metabolic hypotheses. The following Note will also furnish the materials for extending Analytical Dynamics so that it may apply to a space whose geometry is metabolic.

SECOND ADDITIONAL NOTE

PLANETARY MOTION FOR THE METABOLIC HYPOTHESES

THE difficulties introduced into the Newtonian theory of planetary orbits by the adoption of either of the metabolic hypotheses of space are far from insuperable. Let us assume $\frac{\mu}{k^2} \operatorname{cosec}^2 \frac{r}{k}$ as the law of gravitational force, for the elliptic hypothesis. We can then prove that the polar equation of a planetary orbit, with the sun for pole, and an apsidal distance d for axis, is simply

$$\frac{\cot \frac{r}{k}}{\cot \frac{d}{k}} = \frac{1 + e \cos \theta}{1 + e} :$$

and that if

$$a = \tan \left(\frac{\text{major axis of orbit}}{2k} \right),$$

then the periodic time is

$$\frac{2\pi}{\sqrt{\mu}} \frac{(ak)^{\frac{3}{2}}}{1 + a^2}.$$

[For the Hyperbolic Hypothesis,

$$\frac{\coth \frac{r}{K}}{\coth \frac{d}{K}} = \frac{1 + e \cos \theta}{1 + e} ;$$

periodic time,

$$\frac{2\pi}{\sqrt{\mu}} \frac{(aK)^{\frac{3}{2}}}{1 - a^2},$$

where

$$a = \tanh \left(\frac{\text{major axis of orbit}}{2K} \right).$$

In what follows we adhere to the Elliptic Hypothesis. The results obtained in the First Note (page 55) give for the radial velocity: $\dot{r}$; and for the transverse velocity: $k \sin \dfrac{r}{k} \dot{\theta}$; in the case of a particle whose polar coordinates are (r, θ).

Applying the usual method, we find for the increase of radial velocity in time dt from P to P'

$$\ddot{r}dt - k \sin \frac{r}{k} \dot{\theta} \cos \omega,$$

where ω is the angle made with OP by the perpendicular to OP' at P'.

But $\cos \omega = \cos \dfrac{OP'}{k} \sin POP' = \cos \dfrac{r}{k} . d\theta = \cos \dfrac{r}{k} \dot{\theta} . dt$, to the first order, by the last formula on page xviii above. Thus the radial acceleration is

$$\ddot{r} - k \sin \frac{r}{k} \cos \frac{r}{k} . \dot{\theta}^2 \dots\dots\dots\dots\dots(I).$$

Similarly again the increase of transverse velocity in time dt is

$$\frac{d}{dt}\left(k \sin \frac{r}{k} \dot{\theta} \right) . dt + \dot{r} \cos \omega',$$

where ω' is the angle made with OP' by the perpendicular to OP at P.

But $\qquad \cos \omega' = \cos \dfrac{OP}{k} . d\theta = \cos \dfrac{r}{k} \dot{\theta} \, dt \qquad$ **(page xviii)**.

Hence the transverse acceleration is

$$k \operatorname{cosec} \frac{r}{k} \frac{d}{dt}\left(\sin^2 \frac{r}{k} \dot{\theta} \right) \dots\dots\dots\dots(II).$$

It is clear also that if ϕ is the inclination of the velocity v to the radius r,

$$\tan \phi = k \sin \frac{r}{k} \frac{\dot{\theta}}{\dot{r}} \dots\dots\dots\dots\dots(III).$$

The areal velocity is

$$k^2\left(1 - \cos \frac{r}{k} \right) \dot{\theta} \dots\dots\dots\dots(IV). \; .$$

And the kinetic energy of a particle of mass m is

$$\tfrac{1}{2}\, m \left(\dot{r}^2 + k^2 \sin^2 \frac{r}{k}\, \dot{\theta}^2 \right) \ldots\ldots\ldots\ldots\ldots (V).$$

Thus for a particle of unit mass acted upon only by a radial force R towards the origin,

$$\ddot{r} - k \sin \frac{r}{k} \cos \frac{r}{k}\, \dot{\theta}^2 = -R,$$

$$k \operatorname{cosec} \frac{r}{k} \frac{d}{dt} \left(\sin^2 \frac{r}{k}\, \dot{\theta} \right) = 0.$$

Hence $k^2 \sin^2 \dfrac{r}{k}\, \dot{\theta} = h$, where h is a constant for the orbit ; and the energy-equation is found to be

$$\dot{r}^2 + k^2 \sin^2 \frac{r}{k}\, \dot{\theta}^2 = C - 2 \int^r R\, dr.$$

It appears that if a metabolic hypothesis of space holds good, equal areas are not described in equal times in central orbits. What transverse force must be introduced for the retention of the Newtonian Law? If we are to secure that

$$\left(1 - \cos \frac{r}{k} \right) \dot{\theta} = H,$$

the transverse force is determined by the value of the transverse acceleration to be

$$k \operatorname{cosec} \frac{r}{k} \frac{d}{dt} \left(\sin^2 \frac{r}{k}\, \dot{\theta} \right)$$

$$= kH \operatorname{cosec} \frac{r}{k} \frac{d}{dt} \left(1 + \cos \frac{r}{k} \right)$$

$$= -H\dot{r} \,;$$

so that there must be a transverse retardation proportional to the radial velocity. This would not be produced by frictional forces of the usual kind.

Considering now the earth's orbit about the sun, let us assume $R = \dfrac{\mu}{k^2} \operatorname{cosec}^2 \dfrac{r}{k}$, corresponding to the law of potential (extended from Poisson's):

$$\frac{d^2V}{dr^2} + \frac{2}{k} \cot \frac{r}{k} \frac{dV}{dr} + 4\pi\rho = 0,$$

where ρ is the density of a material medium.

Then when we substitute $\dot{\theta} = \dfrac{h}{k^2} \operatorname{cosec}^2 \dfrac{r}{k}$, the equation of energy becomes

$$\dot{r}^2 + \frac{h^2}{k^2} \operatorname{cosec}^2 \frac{r}{k} - \frac{2\mu}{k} \cot \frac{r}{k} = 2E, \text{ say.}$$

Thus
$$dt = \frac{dr}{\sqrt{2E + \dfrac{2\mu}{k} \cot \dfrac{r}{k} - \dfrac{h^2}{k^2} \operatorname{cosec}^2 \dfrac{r}{k}}} ;$$

whence
$$d\theta = \frac{\dfrac{h}{k^2} \operatorname{cosec}^2 \dfrac{r}{k} \, dr}{\sqrt{2E + \dfrac{2\mu}{k} \cot \dfrac{r}{k} - \dfrac{h^2}{k^2} \operatorname{cosec}^2 \dfrac{r}{k}}} .$$

Write conveniently ϖ for $\dfrac{1}{k} \cot \dfrac{r}{k}$, then

$$\theta - \alpha = \int^{\varpi} \frac{d\varpi}{\sqrt{\left(\dfrac{2E}{h^2} - \dfrac{1}{k^2} + \dfrac{\mu^2}{h^4}\right) - \left(\varpi - \dfrac{\mu}{h^2}\right)^2}} .$$

Write also σ for $\varpi - \dfrac{\mu}{h^2}$, and f^2 for $\dfrac{2E}{h^2} - \dfrac{1}{k^2} + \dfrac{\mu^2}{h^4}$, then

$$\theta - \alpha = \int^{\sigma} \frac{d\sigma}{\sqrt{f^2 - \sigma^2}},$$

and so
$$\sigma = f \cos(\theta - \alpha).$$

If we measure θ from the apsidal line, and write d, u for an apsidal distance and corresponding velocity, then

$$h = ku \sin \frac{d}{k}, \quad 2E = u^2 - \frac{2\mu}{k} \cot \frac{d}{k}.$$

Thus

$$f = \frac{1}{k}\cot\frac{d}{k} - \frac{\mu}{u^2 k^2}\operatorname{cosec}^2\frac{d}{k};$$

and we get

$$\cot\frac{r}{k} - \frac{\mu}{u^2 k}\operatorname{cosec}^2\frac{d}{k} = \left(\cot\frac{d}{k} - \frac{\mu}{u^2 k}\operatorname{cosec}^2\frac{d}{k}\right)\cos\theta.$$

Now write

$$e = \frac{u^2 k}{\mu}\sin\frac{d}{k}\cos\frac{d}{k} - 1,$$

so that e is positive or negative according as the centripetal force at the apse is less or greater than for the description of a circle; then

$$(1 + e)\,\frac{\cot\dfrac{r}{k}}{\cot\dfrac{d}{k}} = 1 + e\cos\theta,$$

the equation of the earth's orbit about the sun, if space is of finite extent.

The equation of this orbit in Escherich's coordinates, with a suitable change of origin along the apsidal line, is reducible to the form

$$\frac{x^2}{a^2} + \frac{y^2}{b^2} = 1;$$

so that the orbit has a geometrical centre.

The curve then exhibits several properties, precisely analogous to those of the ellipse in parabolic geometry, obtainable by formulae I–IV of the First Note.

Three of these properties may be indicated thus:

$$(1)\qquad SP + S'P = AA',$$

$$(2)\quad \sin\frac{SP}{k}\operatorname{cosec}\frac{PM}{k} = \text{constant},$$

$$(3)\quad \sin\frac{SY}{k}\sin\frac{S'Y'}{k} = \text{constant}.$$

If now we write $a = \tan\left(\dfrac{\text{major axis of orbit}}{2k}\right)$, we have the formula analogous to a well-known result in Newtonian dynamics:

$$v^2 = \frac{\mu}{k}\left(2\cot\frac{r}{k} - \frac{1-a^2}{a}\right).$$

Let us proceed further to find the periodic time in the orbit, T; that is, the length of the year if space is of finite extent.

Since $\dot\theta = \dfrac{h}{k^2}\left(1 + \cot^2\dfrac{r}{k}\right)$, we have by use of the polar equation of the orbit found above

$$\frac{h\cot^2\dfrac{d}{k}}{k^2(1+e)^2} \cdot T = \int_0^{2\pi} \frac{d\theta}{(1+e)^2\tan^2\dfrac{d}{k} + (1 + e\cos\theta)^2}.$$

In addition to a as defined already, let us introduce $c = \tan\dfrac{CS}{k}$, where C is the centre of symmetry and S the centre of force for the orbit.

Then the four following equivalences are true:

$$u^2 = \frac{\mu}{k}\frac{a+c}{a-c}\frac{1+a^2}{a}, \quad h^2 = \frac{\mu k}{a}\frac{a^2-c^2}{1+c^2},$$

$$\cot\frac{d}{k} = \frac{1+ac}{a-c}, \qquad e = \frac{c}{a}\frac{1+a^2}{1+c^2}.$$

The value of T can now be transformed thus:

$$\sqrt{\mu}\left(\frac{a}{k}\right)^{\frac{3}{2}}\left(\frac{1+c^2}{a^2-c^2}\right)^{\frac{3}{2}} \cdot T = \int_0^{2\pi} \frac{d\theta}{\left\{\dfrac{a^2-c^2}{a(1+c^2)}\right\}^2 + \left\{1 + \dfrac{c}{a}\dfrac{1+a^2}{1+c^2}\cos\theta\right\}^2}.$$

It is therefore necessary to evaluate the definite integral

$$\int_0^{2\pi} \frac{d\theta}{P^2 + (Q + R\cos\theta)^2},$$

where

$$P \equiv \frac{a^2-c^2}{a(1+c^2)}, \quad Q \equiv 1, \quad R \equiv \frac{c}{a}\frac{1+a^2}{1+c^2}.$$

Express then this integral as the difference of two conjugate integrals·

$$\frac{1}{2iP}\left\{\int_0^{2\pi}\frac{d\theta}{R\cos\theta+Q-iP}-\int_0^{2\pi}\frac{d\theta}{R\cos\theta+Q+iP}\right\},$$

each of which may be evaluated by the application of Cauchy's Theorem to a contour in the z-plane ($z=e^{i\theta}$), consisting of a circle of unit radius about the origin.

Thus

$$\int_0^{2\pi}\frac{d\theta}{R\cos\theta+Q-iP}=\frac{2}{iR}\int\frac{dz}{z^2+2\dfrac{Q-iP}{R}z+1},$$

where the second integral is along the unit-circle in the z-plane.

Now $z^2+2\dfrac{Q-iP}{R}z+1$ is identically equal to

$$\left(z+\frac{Q-iP}{R}+\frac{H}{R}e^{-i\omega}\right)\left(z+\frac{Q-iP}{R}-\frac{H}{R}e^{-i\omega}\right),$$

where $H^4\equiv(Q^2-R^2-P^2)^2+(2PQ)^2$, and $\tan 2\omega\equiv\dfrac{2PQ}{Q^2-R^2-P^2}$.

The product of the moduli of the poles (α,β) of the integral is unity, since $\alpha\beta=1$; and therefore only one of these poles lies within the unit-circle.

Moreover, the integrand

$$\frac{1}{z^2+2\dfrac{Q-iP}{R}z+1}$$

$$=\frac{Re^{i\omega}}{2H}\left\{\frac{1}{z+\dfrac{Q-iP}{R}-\dfrac{H}{R}e^{-i\omega}}-\frac{1}{z+\dfrac{Q-iP}{R}+\dfrac{H}{R}e^{-i\omega}}\right\}·$$

Hence, by Cauchy's Theorem, inasmuch as there is but one simple pole within $|z|=1$, the contour-integral above has the value

$$\frac{2}{iR}\cdot 2\pi i\,\frac{Re^{i\omega}}{2H}=\frac{2\pi}{H}e^{i\omega}.$$

Hence also

$$\int_0^{2\pi} \frac{d\theta}{R\cos\theta + Q + iP} = \frac{2\pi}{H} e^{-i\omega}.$$

Therefore

$$\int_0^{2\pi} \frac{d\theta}{P^2 + (Q + R\cos\theta)^2} = \frac{2\pi}{2iPH}(e^{i\omega} - e^{-i\omega})$$

$$= \frac{2\pi}{PH}\sin\omega.$$

Thus

$$\int_0^{2\pi} \frac{d\theta}{\sqrt{\left\{\dfrac{a^2 - c^2}{a(1 + c^2)}\right\}^2 + \left\{1 + \dfrac{c}{a}\dfrac{1 + a^2}{1 + c^2}\cos\theta\right\}^2}}$$

$$= \frac{2\pi a}{(1 + a^2)^{\frac{1}{2}}} \cdot \frac{a(1 + c^2)}{a^2 - c^2} \cdot \frac{a(1 + c^2)^{\frac{1}{2}}}{(a^2 - c^2)^{\frac{1}{2}}(1 + a^2)^{\frac{1}{2}}}$$

$$= \frac{2\pi a^3 (1 + c^2)^{\frac{3}{2}}}{(1 + a^2)(a^2 - c^2)^{\frac{3}{2}}}.$$

Finally,

$$T = \frac{2\pi}{\sqrt{\mu}}\frac{(ak)^{\frac{3}{2}}}{1 + a^2}.$$

If the straight line had a complete length as great as 25,000 light-years, the quantitative difference between the length of the year deduced from this formula and the Newtonian result for Euclidean space would be an inconceivably small fraction of a second.

But the formal difference between the old and new results is considerable.

POSTSCRIPT

It will be observed that by use of the formula

$$\int_0^{2\pi} \frac{d\theta}{\cos\theta + \omega} = \frac{2\pi}{(\omega^2 - 1)^{\frac{1}{2}}},$$

the preceding analysis may be more rapidly worked out as follows :

$$\frac{\frac{1}{2}(1 + a^2)^2 \, ac^2}{(ka)^{\frac{3}{2}} (a^2 - c^2)^{\frac{3}{2}} (1 + c^2)^{\frac{1}{2}}} \cdot T = \int_0^{2\pi} \frac{d\theta}{\left(\cos\theta + \dfrac{a}{c}\dfrac{1 + c^2}{1 + a^2}\right)^2 + \dfrac{(a^2 - c^2)^2}{c^2(1 + a^2)^2}}$$

$$= \frac{1}{2i} \frac{c(1 + a^2)}{a^2 - c^2} \int_0^{2\pi} \left[\frac{d\theta}{\cos\theta + \dfrac{a(1 + c^2) - i(a^2 - c^2)}{c(1 + a^2)}} \right.$$

$$\left. - \frac{d\theta}{\cos\theta + \dfrac{a(1 + c^2) + i(a^2 - c^2)}{c(1 + a^2)}} \right]$$

$$= \frac{1}{2i} \frac{c(1 + a^2)}{a^2 - c^2} \left[\frac{2\pi c(1 + ia)}{(a^2 - c^2)^{\frac{1}{2}}(1 + c^2)^{\frac{1}{2}}} - \frac{2\pi c(1 - ia)}{(a^2 - c^2)^{\frac{1}{2}}(1 + c^2)^{\frac{1}{2}}} \right]$$

$$= \frac{2\pi ac^2(1 + a^2)}{(a^2 - c^2)^{\frac{3}{2}}(1 + c^2)^{\frac{1}{2}}},$$

which furnishes the desired result.